Getting Your Ideas Across

Geoffrey Moss

KOGAN
PAGE

Acknowledgements

My thanks to all my colleagues and friends, in many countries, who have helped me over the years. A special thanks to my wife Joyce for editing my script.

First published in New Zealand in 1989 by Moss Associates Ltd, 7 Dorset Way, Wadestown, Wellington.

This edition first published in Great Britain in 1993 by Kogan Page Ltd, 120 Pentonville Road, London N1 9JN.

British Library Cataloguing in Publication Data

A CIP record for this book is available from the British Library.

ISBN 0–7494–0909–6

Typeset by Saxon Graphics Ltd, Derby
Printed and bound in Great Britain by Biddles Ltd, Guildford and King's Lynn

◀ CONTENTS ▶

◀ PREFACE ▶

If you want to be successful, read this book.
If you want to be persuasive, read this book.
If you want to influence others, read this book.

'What is the best way to get your ideas across to people?' I have asked people in many countries this question. Some answer dogmatically 'Television' or 'Newspapers' or 'Face-to-face contacts'. But the thinkers usually agree that there is no best way. 'It all depends on the habits of the people, their background, their education, their environment, their experiences.' Your own credibility is important too.

This book will give you helpful guidelines. It deals with the skills of communication and is full of tips and ideas to help you get your ideas across to target groups. If your job is to guide and influence others and you would like to do it better, this book is for you.

To be a successful communicator you must be able to get to your feet and talk with confidence, write simply and clearly, know correct meeting procedures, be able to take notes and above all, get things done. That's what this book is all about. It will get you started and serve as a useful reference. It is also a reminder book to be consulted before you prepare your next speech, chair your next meeting or organise your next conference.

Over 4500 years ago the Egyptian sage Ptahhotpe (Ta-ho-ta-pe) wrote:

'I have abstracted five canons of rhetoric: keeping silent, waiting for the right moment to speak, restraining passionate words, speaking fluently but with great deliberation, and above all, keeping your tongue at one with your heart so that you speak the truth.

'These five types of behaviour create one's ethos.'

Fashions come and fashions go but principles and maxims never change. If you want guidelines search for principles and maxims.

◄ PART 1 ►

BECOME A BETTER LISTENER

After you have read this part of the book you should be able to identify your bad listening habits and know how to overcome them.

You will learn the ten commandments of good listening, the basics of reflective listening and how to get the most out of a lecture.

◀ 1. ▶

BECOME A BETTER LISTENER

'Two men were walking along a crowded street in a busy city. Suddenly one exclaimed, "Listen to the sound of that cricket!" but the other could not hear it. He asked his companion how he could hear the sound of a cricket amidst the din of the city traffic. The first man was a zoologist and had trained himself to listen to the voices of nature. He did not explain. He took a coin from his pocket and dropped it on the pavement. Many people began to look around. "We hear," he said, "what we listen for."'

Bhagwan Shree Rajneesh

'Nature has given man one tongue, but two ears, that we may hear from each other twice as much as we speak.'

Epictetus

'A student asked his professor, "Sir, what are the secrets of the art of good conversation?"'

'The professor held up one finger and said, "There is one secret. Listen!"'

'After a long silence the student said, "Well, I am listening."'

'"And that is the secret," said the professor.'

Listening is an active skill, involving more senses than just the ears. It is a skill that can be developed but you must work at it and apply it to get maximum benefit.

Listening is a creative force that can influence people. When we are listened to, our ideas begin to unfold and grow within us. We tend to move towards friends who listen to us. When we are listened

9

to, even by strangers, we feel happier and more secure. Listening is often confused with hearing. Any normal healthy person can 'hear'. Listening requires a great deal of concentration and increased energy. Our progress in life depends largely on our mastery of listening skills. We grow into our listening habits – rarely are we trained to listen.

We have developed electronic systems to send messages around the world and to outer space, yet there are times when we cannot listen to what our own children are trying to tell us. Mothers cannot talk to daughters, fathers with sons, blacks with whites, labour with management. We do not hear what they are trying to tell us.

Research tells us that busy executives spend about four-fifths of their work time listening and yet they still don't absorb half of what is said. Most workers receive half their pay for listening yet companies rarely pay attention to training in listening skills.

Many surveys have been carried out to find out the characteristics of a good boss. Usually listening skills top the list, with comments such as 'I like my boss. I can talk to her. She listens to me.'

If you are prepared to make a commitment to improve your listening skills you will become a better boss, a better parent, a better citizen and a better friend. You cannot switch from being a poor listener simply by deciding to change, or by reading a book about listening.

The remedy begins with awareness and ends with determination and concentration. The first thing to do is to turn listening from an unconscious activity into a conscious one. Don't get overwhelmed by the size of the task. Start by becoming aware of listening habits. Identify your bad habits and try to correct them, one at a time, from the remedies given in this book. You must be objective about your weaknesses. Be prepared to make an effort to overcome them and continue working at them. Make time to contemplate and evaluate your progress. If you can achieve some small improvement each day, the next day's effort will be easier and better.

You can become a better listener if you really want to. It's over to you. The rewards are great. They might even change your life.

Identify your poor listening habits

Sit down quietly by yourself and read this list of poor listening habits.

Develop good listening habits.

1. *Lack of concentration.* Do you often daydream and fail to hear a speaker?

2. *Poor posture.* Do you slouch and relax in your chair instead of keeping alert?

3. *Prejudging the speaker and the subject* – 'I have heard it all before.' Do you ever 'tune out' because you are not interested in a subject or you think the speaker is boring?

4. *Laziness.* Are you too lazy to make an effort to understand difficult and technical presentations?

5. *Emotional 'blackouts'.* Do you become emotional over certain words or phrases? Do you stop listening fully or 'black out' because of preconceived ideas and previous experiences?

6. *Obsessive note taking.* Do you take copious notes and, in the process, get behind so you lose the thread of the talk and miss important facts and principles?

7. *Debating mentally with the speaker.* Do you waste time arguing mentally with the speaker or concentrating on a question to ask later?

8. *Faking attention.* Do you try to impress others by pretending to listen when you are really daydreaming?

9. *Wasting time.* Do you waste the time between the speaker's speech and the speed of your thoughts or do you summarise, review and question the topic?

10. *Creating distractions.* Do you comment to your neighbour? Do you doodle or read when you should be listening?

11. *Tolerating distractions.* Are you easily distracted by noises and people moving about?

12. *Lack of empathy with the speaker.* Do you never pretend to be the speaker? Do you never put yourself in the speaker's place?

13. *Failure to listen for feelings.* Do you just hear words and fail to listen for feelings, distortions and voice inflections?

Improve your listening skills

Concentration is essential to good listening.

Now take each numbered item above and analyse your listening habits in more detail. Grade yourself using a 0 to 10 scale. This will permit you to identify your main deficiencies and set your priorities. Be honest – you must identify your weaknesses before you can improve your listening skills. For example:

Concentration

0 ......1 ......2 ......3 ......4 ......5 ......6 ......7 ......8 ......9 10
Very poor   Fair   Excellent

Decide which weakness you want to work on first. Write yourself notes about this weakness – in a notebook, in your diary, on the back of a visiting card or in your spectacle case – somewhere you look often. Use these notes as constant reminders and work hard at remedying the weakness. When you feel you have improved, regrade yourself and if you have made good progress, move on to strengthen another weakness.

Each of the above items is now discussed in turn.

1. Lack of concentration

Do not daydream.

Does your mind wander? Do you lack concentration? Do you tune in and out? Do you play with ideas for a while, before returning to the speaker for another bit of information? Do you daydream? Give yourself a grade – be honest!

Remedy

Draw up your own set of instructions. Here are some guidelines. I must make a greater effort to listen. I must ask myself questions:

- What is the speaker trying to say?
- What are the main points the speaker is making?
- How does the speaker know that?
- What's the evidence?
- Where's the speaker heading?
- What is the body language saying?
- What's been said so far?
- What have I learnt?
- What's new?
- How can I use this information?
- What's in this talk for me?
- How will I benefit?

Write down your personal memory joggers and questions. Carry them with you. When you are listening to a talk keep asking yourself questions, and:

- try to anticipate what the speaker will say
- focus on the message – search for deeper meanings
- recapitulate – review what has been said
- ask questions for amplification and as a memory aid.

Objectivity is the crucial element in effective listening. Pretend you are a reporter listening on behalf of a wide audience. Pick out the main points which would be of the greatest interest to most people.

You can improve your concentration by pretending to report for others and by constantly asking yourself questions. This type of listening is hard work and it can be tiring but try it and you will be surprised at how much more you learn and how much more you will remember.

2. Poor posture

Many people slump in their seats at lectures or meetings, lean their head in their hands or get a glazed look in their eyes. Speakers respond to listeners who look at them with bright eyes, remain alert, make encouraging sounds and ask intelligent questions – questions that tell the speaker you are interested, questions that encourage the speaker to give additional information. Listening is a demanding activity, so keep alert.

Sit up straight and stay alert. The speaker responds to such attention.

Remedy

Don't slouch or slump in your chair. Sit up, be alert and look as if you expect an interesting, exciting talk. The speaker will respond to your encouragement and often give a more animated, interesting presentation.

3. Prejudging the speaker and the subject

Do not dismiss a speaker's message simply because his or her appearance is unimpressive.

Some speakers have 'charisma', an extraordinary personal power or charm that excites us and makes us want to listen. Other speakers leave us bored and disinterested. We dismiss them for many reasons – their presentation, their appearance, their speech or their annoying mannerisms. Sometimes it is the subject that bores us. 'I have heard it all before – so what's new?'

Do you dismiss the subject as being uninteresting? Do you dismiss the speaker as being boring? If so, you are sure to 'tune out' and start daydreaming or thinking about your work or personal problems.

Remedy

Try concentrating on the message. Look for new angles and twists to old tales.

Don't judge people by their appearance. If speakers can make you think or give you new ideas, it doesn't matter what they look like. Remember, people like Albert Einstein and Gandhi were unimpressive in appearance but had important messages that changed the world. So be prepared to make an effort to listen for new ideas.

4. Laziness

Make the effort to understand 'difficult' explanations.

Do you avoid difficult technical lectures? Do you daydream, lack concentration, only half listen? Are you too lazy to make an effort to listen to a difficult topic?

Remedy

Before a difficult lecture, discuss the topic with a knowledgeable friend or colleague. Ask for an explanation of meanings, theories, principles etc. Then read about the topic. A small effort will increase your comprehension and interest in what you thought was a hard, boring subject.

5. Emotional blackouts

The biggest problem in listening is failing to concentrate on what we are hearing. There are many physical distractions, but emotional distractions are also important.

Some people, some words, some experiences, can stir emotions and cause listening blackouts. Try not to overreact because of prejudices or emotional words until you have heard the whole story. Words like 'abortion' and 'drugs' can arouse strong emotions. We start to debate ideas which differ from our own convictions so we don't hear what the speaker says later.

Try not to withdraw your attention because the speaker uses an emotive word which sets off a debate in your head.

Remedy

For two or three weeks, carry a notebook and record words, opinions and ideas which upset you or make you angry. Also, note the names of people who upset you. Then, as objectively as possible, try grading your reactions to those people, words or ideas using a 0 to 10 scale.

0 ......1 ......2 ......3 ......4 ......5 ......6 ......7 ......8 ......9 10
Like   Dislike   Annoying Upsetting Very angry

If you find you are marking 5 or above, try this corrective treatment. Take a business card and write these four words on the back of it:

```
LISTEN NOW:
ARGUE LATER
```

Make a conscious effort whenever you hear words or ideas which upset you to listen carefully to the other point of view. Carry the card in your pocket, briefcase or handbag until you feel you can curb your emotions. Concentrate on letting people tell you their whole story. Let them finish giving their ideas or developing their arguments. Try to be tolerant and control your urge to interrupt and so stifle the other person's thoughts. If you try to understand their point of view first, you can then present your ideas calmly and logically.

6. Obsessive note taking

Do not take so many notes that you fail to follow the argument. Practise good note-taking skills.

It has been proved many times that people who take notes have better recall but there is an art to note taking. If you get involved with details, you cannot keep up with the speaker and you lose the thread of the talk.

Remedy

Jot down key points only, in two columns:

1. Facts   2. Principles

Listen and watch for interpretations the speaker gives to the facts. Forget detailed notes unless there are some aspects or details of new material you want to explore further. If necessary, ask the speaker for a copy of the talk.

You can save much time by learning shorthand or even developing your own form of shorthand.

You can abbreviate words by writing them as they sound, using as few letters as necessary for recognition. For example:

Hi – high
Lo – Low
Nu – knew
Bk – book

Sometimes you can use letters to substitute for words.

C – sea
I – eye
Q – queue
T – tea.

The following symbols are suggested for the nine most used words in the English language.

Te – the
^ – of
& – and
2 – to
. – a
n – in
tt – that
t – it
z – is

7. Debating mentally with the speaker

We tend to look for weaknesses in arguments, especially if we are knowledgeable about a particular aspect of the topic, or have had experience in that area.

One minor weakness in an argument can start a mental debate. We spend the next few minutes phrasing and rephrasing a question to show how clever we are. As a result, we miss the rest of the talk or at least large parts of it as we tune in and out.

Have you ever asked a question at a meeting and the speaker says, 'I have already dealt with that topic'? It's most embarrassing. Very often this is the result of mental debating – you were busy preparing a question or comment and missed the speaker's explanation.

Check that the speaker deals with your mental queries before question time; *then* **raise the points that bother you.**

Remedy

The remedy is simple. Jot down a few words to remind you about the point you wish to discuss – then concentrate on the speaker.

At the end of the talk, you can prepare your question and ask it (if it has not already been asked) or add appropriate comments.

8. Faking attention

Do you ever try to impress the people around you by pretending to listen? Do you take up poses and postures which you think show you are listening?

The mere act of pretending may require as much effort as listening and the only person you are really fooling is yourself. There is no sense in making this effort and remembering nothing.

Spurious attention takes such an effort to maintain that you are unlikely to listen carefully.

Remedy

Imagine you are the speaker. Try to analyse your reactions when you realise your 'listeners' are only pretenders. If they don't hear what you are saying, what's the point of your talk?

Either make an effort to listen and learn, or walk out of the lecture – don't waste your time and the lecturer's.

9. Wasting time

It is possible to withdraw attention and yet take in all the message.

In the 1940s Dr Harry Goldstein at Columbia University in the USA proved it was possible to listen to speech at a rate more than three times that at which we normally hear it, without any significant loss of comprehension. This 'spare time' is often spent daydreaming or digressing.

Remedy

Instead of wasting this time, use it to reinforce the speaker's message. Summarise and question the contents of the talk. Try predicting future comments. Try to use the time to reinforce the message.

10. Creating distractions

Resist the temptation to fidget or otherwise distract attention from the speaker.

Even if you are tempted, don't comment to your neighbour or carry on discussions during a talk. Don't shuffle papers or read reports. Resist the temptation to doodle. Don't fool yourself into thinking you can doodle and listen to a speaker at the same time. At first you may draw only a few lines but soon you will become so intrigued with your artistic doodles that you won't hear what is being said.

Remedy

Remove all temptations such as extra pencils and pieces of paper. Resolve to write down only important facts, figures and principles. Take a pride in clean, tidy notes – they will make your life easier.

11. Tolerating distractions

Try to avoid possible distraction caused by others.

Are you easily distracted by people moving around the room, traffic outside the window, fidgety or talkative neighbours or a speaker with annoying mannerisms? You don't have to tolerate such distractions.

Remedy

Select a seat where you will not be easily distracted. Sit near the front, close to the speaker, out of the sun, and with your back to the window and a good view of the visual aid screen. If you sit at the rear of an auditorium, people are more likely to chat to you. Don't talk to your neighbours during a lecture – asides waste their time and yours. Do not read or doodle. Concentrate on what the speaker is saying and make brief notes.

12. Lack of empathy with the speaker

It's easy to reject the speaker because of clothing, hair style, voice tone, language, background or different beliefs.

A speaker may be 'dismissed' because of appearance, origins or beliefs.

Don't waste time criticising the speaker's delivery. Even if the presentation is poor, the message might be very important.

People envious of the speaker's success are often poor listeners because they are constantly looking for faults.

Remedy
Try to understand the speaker's point of view – be tolerant.

Try mental manipulation – talk to yourself. 'She must know a great deal otherwise she wouldn't have been invited to be the guest speaker.' 'I must try not to criticise the speaker's delivery. The message is more important than her hair style and those inappropriate clothes.' 'If I had been asked to speak what would I have talked about?'

The key to good listening is to ask, 'How can I use this information?'

Sift and sort the 'wheat' from the 'chaff'. Hunt for worthwhile ideas, and facts that you can use. Try pretending you are the speaker and ask yourself, 'If I had to give this talk next week, what changes would I make?'

13. Failure to listen for feelings

Listening is more than hearing with your ears. Try listening for cues and clues about the speaker's feelings. Listen for voice inflections. A speaker may stress certain points loudly and clearly and mumble others. Hesitations, facial expressions, postures, hand gestures, eye movements, shallow breathing and even perspiring are all part of the message. Style of dress and the speaker's grooming also help the listener to interpret the message.

Body language is as important as what is said. Look for non-verbal signals.

19

Psychologist Albert Mehrabian has carried out research on what happens when one person talks to another. He finds that only 7 per cent of a message's effect is carried by words; 93 per cent reaches the listener non-verbally, through facial expressions, vocal intonations, and so on.

We are giving out non-verbal signals all the time. These put feelings into words, as lovers know when they look into each other's eyes. A shrug of the shoulders, a single tear drop, a grimace – all communicate feelings non-verbally.

Listen for signs of tension. There is a close relationship between emotional states and vocal characteristics. A tense voice is pitched high. The delivery is usually rapid and the voice is often husky. Listen for the pattern of pauses. A very nervous person may start to 'dry up' or stutter.

Listen for 'telling' words, ones that give away secrets. Some 'telling' words may be devices to get attention, or they may mean the opposite to what is being said.

Speakers often use the expression, 'By the way', or 'Before I forget', to give the impression that an idea had just come to them and is unimportant. But what they have to say is often very important. When you hear the phrases, 'To be honest with you ....' 'Honestly ....' ' or 'Frankly speaking ....', the chances are the speaker is not being honest with you. Watch for a cover-up when you hear such phrases. 'Naturally' and 'Of course' imply that the listener should agree with the speaker. Don't be lulled into such thinking. Make up your own mind!

Remedy
- Listen for feelings.
- Listen for voice inflections and signs of tension.
- Listen carefully for telling words.
- Listen for distortions.

Next time you are in a library, borrow a book on body language, 'people-watching' or human relations. There are many good books on these subjects. Make a list of things to watch out for so that you can interpret non-verbal cues and clues. Keep your list small. Remember, 'Words don't have meanings; people have meanings for words.'

◀ 2. ▶

GETTING STARTED

How do you start to become a better listener?

Saying 'I am going to become a better listener' can be overwhelming. Instead say, 'Just for today, I am going to make an effort to listen.' If you can make today an achieving day, tomorrow's effort will be easier and better. As you gain confidence, read the section on bad listening habits and try out some of the techniques suggested to overcome them. By spending a little time each day on improving your listening skills you will improve your relations with other people, you will learn more and you will become a better parent, friend and boss.

Consciously practise listening skills.

Checking up on your progress

From time to time, ask friends and family some direct questions about your listening habits. If you are not brave enough to ask them face to face, write the questions down. They could include such questions as:

Periodically check your listening skills with others.

'Do I give my full attention to you when we talk?'

'Do you feel comfortable talking to me?'

'Do I tend to dominate our discussions?'

You could ask friends to mark you on a 0–10 scale. Don't be upset with a low grade. The remedy is in your own hands.

'If you love to listen, you will gain knowledge and, if you incline your ear, you will become wise.'

Sirach

No matter how eloquent you are, you will please people more by listening than talking.

'The great charm of conversation consists less in the display of one's wit and intelligence than in the power to draw forth the resources of others.'

Bruyère

Read *A Practical Guide to Effective Listening* by Diane Bone (Kogan Page).

◀ 3. ▶

ASK OPEN-ENDED QUESTIONS

If you want to be a good listener, concentrate on asking interesting questions, questions that draw speakers out.

Practise asking open-ended questions. 'How did you get started in your job?', 'Why did you take up teaching as a career?', 'What were the highlights of your study tour?' Such questions encourage speakers and help to put them at ease. Even remarks such as 'Tell me more about your hobby. How did you get started?' show you were listening and 'draw out' more information from the speaker.

'Closed' questions, on the other hand, get specific, concise answers. 'Where were you born?', 'Where do you live?', 'How long have you worked here?' are examples of closed questions which rarely get more than a few words in reply.

After your next few interviews or discussions, record the questions you asked. Were they open-ended or closed questions?

0 ......1 ......2 ......3 ......4 ......5 ......6 ......7 ......8 ......9 10
All closed   Mixed   All open questions

If you have a low grade, concentrate on asking more open-ended questions.

Open-ended questions encourage people to talk. Closed questions often require only a one-word answer, usually 'Yes' or 'No', which ends the communication.

Summary
Next time you interview, prepare an agenda. Jot down a few suitable open-ended questions to make the person think and to draw them out.

First establish rapport

Talk about mutual interests or acquaintances. Ask 'comfortable' questions. 'I see we both belong to the Seaview Golf Club. Do you know many on the committee?'

Ask 'suppose' questions

'Suppose you are the next boss. What's the first thing you would change?'

'Suppose you had an interview with the Prime Minister. What would you tell him or her?'

Ask 'W' questions

If you don't already know Rudyard Kipling's verse, it is well worth memorising:

'I keep six honest serving men
(They taught me all I knew):
Their names are What and Why and When
and How and Where and Who.'

Newswriters find 'Who, what, when, where, why, how and how much?' cover all important aspects of a topic.

Try 'probe' questions

Pick a key word or two from a speaker's statement. 'You said you were not happy about some aspects of .... Why is that?' Then wait for an elaboration.

Ask 'agreement' questions

'How would it be if we tried . . . ?'

Asking appropriate questions encourages speakers and allows them to amplify or develop a topic. If you ask such questions during your next interview, you will be surprised at the extra information you will learn. Unexpected traits and attributes may be revealed, to your advantage.

There's an old saying, 'Ask a dumb question, get a dumb answer.' On the other hand, ask an interesting question and you will get an interesting reply. It's a skill worth developing and, because you will be keen to hear the reply, you will become a better listener.

◄ 4. ►

GET MORE INFORMATION OUT OF A LECTURE

The more you put into attending a lecture the more you will get out of it.

Here are some more helpful hints. By following them you will improve your listening skills and get more out of lectures.

1. Before the lecture
Read as much as you can about the topic.

2. Select your seat carefully
Select a comfortable seat, free of distractions. Make sure you will be able to hear the speaker and see all the visual aids.

3. Give your undivided attention to the speaker
Make a special effort to concentrate on what the speaker is saying. Watch for body language. Listen for areas of interest. Listen for new information. Ask yourself, 'What's in this for me?'

4. Make notes using your own form of shorthand
By jotting down headings you will increase your recall. From tests in many countries it appears note takers have spectacular increases in recall.

A good idea is to draw a line down the middle of your page. Head one side 'Facts' and the other side 'Principles'. Try jotting down brief notes in the appropriate column. This simple method calls for the minimum of writing. Don't write details or you will miss cues.

5. Make an effort to keep an open mind
Be aware of 'emotional blackouts'. Do not stop listening because of your preconceived ideas or your biases.

6. Don't create distractions
Don't talk to your neighbours – no asides. Stop doodling or reading. Concentrate on what you can learn from the speaker.

7. Keep asking yourself questions
Use the five 'W's and two 'H's – Who, what, why, when, where, how and how much?

8. Keep summarising and reviewing
Weigh up the evidence as it unfolds.

9. Ask questions
Don't be frightened to ask questions. There's an old saying: 'He who asks a question is a fool for five minutes – he who does not, remains a fool for ever.'

◀ 5. ▶

MAKE LISTENING MORE INTERESTING

Analytical listening makes listening more interesting.

If you become familiar with some of the techniques of persuasion, you can listen for the speaker's arguments and analyse them. Analytical listening makes listening more interesting.

Examples of persuasive techniques

- *Testimonials by famous people.* Ask yourself, 'Does the person really know anything about the product or argument?'
- *'Everyone else has one; why not you?'* This method tries to influence you to keep up with the neighbours or get on the 'bandwagon'.
- *'I am successful – despite my humble background.'* 'I can show you how to be successful,' or 'You should vote for me – I know all about your problems.'
- *Selection of favourable evidence.* Speakers often use half truths and omit unfavourable evidence. This is called 'card stacking'. Watch out for this method of persuasion.
- *Unsupported claims.* Listen for claims which cannot be supported by proven facts. Don't believe something just because you hear it repeated many times.
- *Common associations.* Watch for the association of a respected or prestigious organisation or sport, with a product. Sport is often associated with spirits or tobacco advertising.
- *Name-calling.* Watch for the speaker denouncing a person or an idea by associating them with things feared, distrusted or despised. The name-caller wants to discredit the person. Politicians frequently use this technique.

- *Exaggerated distinctions.* Often a unique feature of a product or an idea is highlighted and treated as if it is of great value. In fact, it may be of little value or benefit.

Question, question, question!

When you are listening to a speech or television commercial ask yourself these questions.

- How recent is the evidence?
- Is the information pertinent to present conditions?
- Are the quotations relevant?
- Do the 'experts' really know what they are talking about? For example, an actor has been trained to act and sound persuasive, and is not necessarily an authority on the topic.
- An 'expert' in one area is not necessarily an 'expert' in another.
- Not all current statistics are sound. The sample may be too small, incorrectly tabulated or misinterpreted, so the conclusion drawn can be dishonest.
- Does the person or the organisation giving the evidence stand to gain? If so, treat the evidence with suspicion.

Listen hard. Separate the 'wheat' from the 'chaff'. Analytical listening can be enjoyable and can often reveal a great deal about the speaker or the product. Just for fun and for practice, try classifying the persuasive techniques used in television commercials.

◀ 6. ▶

TRY REFLECTIVE LISTENING

If you restate what you heard, but in your own words, you can check whether you heard correctly.

Words have different meanings for different people. From the time we start to talk, we build up our own vocabulary depending on our background, education, travel, the books we read, the people we associate with and who our parents were and where they came from.

To add to our listening problems there are over half a million words in the English language. It is claimed there are 14,000 dictionary meanings for the 500 most frequently used words. Consequently, we can never be sure what we heard was what was actually said. By rephrasing what was said you can check to make sure your interpretation was correct. This restating of what the speaker said is called reflective listening.

There are several basic reflecting skills. Restating words is only one reflecting skill. Another is to paraphrase by focusing on the speaker's content. Another still is to listen for 'feeling' words, and observe signs of emotion and body language. After you have interpreted them try explaining them to mirror the feelings back to the speaker. This can often help the speaker to clarify his or her own thinking by briefly classifying or summarising a long, rambling discussion.

Reflective listening by interpreting, paraphrasing, classifying, summarising and mirroring can stimulate discussion and make listening more accurate, meaningful and acceptable.

Make an effort to practise the art of reflective listening. It makes good sense when you consider some of our peculiarities:

- Different people have different meanings for the same words
- We often get blinded by our emotions
- We tend to distort much of what has been said because of preconceived ideas
- We often get distracted and deviate from our main arguments
- People often 'code' messages by not being precise or by using 'telling' words
- We frequently get emotional about a minor problem when the main issue is a major problem.

Listen hard and be sensitive to what is being said. Repeat, paraphrase, interpret and classify what the speaker has said. This requires intensive involvement but it can be very rewarding.

◀ 7. ▶

TEN COMMANDMENTS FOR GOOD LISTENING

Rules for good listening summarised.

1. Stop talking!
You cannot listen if you are talking – and if you are talking, you are not learning.

2. Put the speaker at ease
Encourage the speaker. Try putting the speaker's feelings into words. 'I am sorry to hear my decision has upset you. I do appreciate what you are telling me. Tell me what we can do about it.'

3. Show that you want to listen
Look and act as if you are interested. Give full attention. Show you are listening. Nod and make encouraging remarks such as, 'Yes, I see what you mean.'

4. Remove distractions
Set up an environment that eliminates distractions. Shut the door, turn off the radio, don't doodle or walk about.

5. Empathise with the speaker
Try to put yourself in the speaker's shoes – try to see his or her point of view. 'Why did she say that? What's the reason? What would I say and do?'

6. Be patient

Allow plenty of time for listening when you make appointments. Don't interrupt. Don't keep looking at your watch.

7. Control your emotions

If you get emotional you will not hear properly – you will get the wrong meanings from words and you could get the wrong message.

8. Go easy on argument and criticism

Ask questions by all means, but don't attack. Try to draw the speaker out. 'Why did you say that? Is that what you really feel? Have you facts to support your statement?' If you put speakers on the defensive they may 'clam up' or get emotional. Avoid arguments.

9. Ask questions

This encourages the speaker and shows you were listening. Ask questions for amplification. It helps to develop a topic. Ask: 'Why do you believe that?' It is surprising what you may learn from a good question.

10. Summarise, review and reflect

From time to time summarise what you think the speaker has said and repeat the speaker's words. This will help the speaker and, by reinforcing the message, you will remember it longer.

◀ PART 2 ▶

IMPROVE YOUR SPEAKING SKILLS

After you have read this part of the book you will know how to prepare and give memorable speeches; how to dress for speaking engagements; how to answer questions and change audience attitudes and how to prepare for radio and television interviews. You will learn which visual aids are the most appropriate for your audience and how to make the best use of them. You will also learn how to make better use of your telephone.

◄ 8. ►

SPEAK UP

'The first step a speaker should take in preparing for a speech is analysing the audience and the occasion.'

'Be still when you have nothing to say; when genuine passion moves you, say what you've got to say, and say it hot.'

D. H. Lawrence

'If you appeal to the beliefs, attitudes and values of your audience – they will listen.'

At the end of the meeting, the secretary asked the speaker. 'How much do we owe you for your expenses?'

'Oh, nothing,' he replied. 'Don't bother about them.'

'That's very kind of you. Thank you. You know, lots of our speakers don't accept expenses. The money we save we put into a special fund – so we can invite better speakers next time.'

How do you become one of those 'better speakers'?

Good speakers can always command an audience. Some 'tricks of the trade' are revealed here.

After you read this you will know some of the 'tricks of the trade' used by many professional speakers. These guidelines and recommendations will help you to do a better job. They will not necessarily make you into a good speaker – that comes only with experience.

I have often asked people to think of a memorable talk and decide why it made an impression on them. Often they remembered talks where the speaker had shared feelings and emotions with them. One person remembered vividly a speaker who spoke about the evils of smoking, after visiting a friend dying of lung cancer. Another person remembered a lecture about family conflict and ways to counsel. Often urgent national issues had been brought into clear focus and solutions offered. Most people seem to remember talks where people show their feelings or give innovative ideas or new information. To summarise:

- Show your feelings
- Give new information
- Share innovative ideas
- Put national issues into focus.

It takes determination and staying power to become a good speaker.

You need determination

Have you heard that old saying. 'The only time you start at the top is when you are digging a hole?'

38

To become a good speaker you must be determined to succeed, set your goal and work towards it. Start by reading aloud – popular novels, poems and famous speeches are a good beginning. You are not the only shy person to be scared of your own voice. Many nervous, shy people have mastered the skills and become great public speakers able to influence large audiences. If you really believe you can succeed, and you are prepared to work at it and practise, you will succeed. Public speaking is a skill like any other, such as learning to drive a car or playing a musical instrument. To become a first-class speaker all you need is time, determination, practice and experience. Perhaps you are saying to yourself. 'That's all very well but where do I get the practice and experience?' Have patience, work at your ambition, don't expect to become a successful speaker overnight.

Speak at every opportunity

Join a speaking course, a debating club or a drama society. Take lessons from a speech teacher. There are many public speaking classes and clubs if you are prepared to make the effort and seek them out. Toastmasters International has clubs in most centres and many countries.

Constant practice pays dividends.

Next time you attend a public meeting and feel strongly about an issue, don't just sit. Jot down the points you want to raise. Then get to your feet and give your opinion or ask a question. It takes courage, but it's a start. You feel good afterwards.

If you are asked to introduce a speaker or pass a vote of thanks, accept the challenge. If you do a good job you will feel you have achieved something worth while and you will be more confident next time.

Read *The Business Guide to Effective Speaking* by Jacqueline Dunckel and Elizabeth Parnham, and *Speak With Confidence* by Meribeth Bunch (Kogan Page).

◀ 9. ▶

ANALYSE YOUR AUDIENCE

Knowledge of the audience enables you to address their interests and level of knowledge more exactly.

Before you start preparing your talk, find out as much as possible about your audience.

Composition

- How many will be present?
- What is the age range?
- Will you be speaking to an all-female audience, an all-male audience or a mixed audience?
- What are their occupations?
- What is their economic position?
- What is their social status?
- What educational levels have they achieved?
- What are their racial or cultural backgrounds?
- Are there any language limitations?
- Is the audience derived from a group membership?

Beliefs, attitudes and values

- Will they have strong prejudices?
- What are their religious beliefs?
- What are their political views?
- What are their values?
- What are the accepted norms in their social behaviour?

- Will they have special interests?
- What will motivate them?

The occasion

- What is the occasion? Why were you asked?
- What are the aims and objectives of the organisation which has invited you to speak?
- What does the audience already know about the subject?
- What will be their attitude towards the speech topic?
- What will be their attitude towards you as a speaker?
- What will they want to hear?
- What message do you want to give them?

When you have the answers to most of these questions, you should know what to aim for in your presentation.

◄ 10. ►

WHAT WILL YOU TALK ABOUT?

Choosing your subject

The subject may be specified. If you have a choice, it is essential to pick a subject that interests both you and the audience, so it is even more important to know who will attend.

Preparing a speech is a complicated task that requires a systematic method. Assume you have been invited to give a talk to a local club. You may have been told what subject they would like to hear. But if they leave the choice to you, make sure it is a subject you are interested in and one you have strong feelings about. Try to reward your listeners. Give them useful, practical, topical information. Make them think. They don't want long-winded, boring talks about things they already know.

Most new speakers make two grave errors – they don't have clear objectives and they try to cover too many points. Putting it another way, they have 'woolly objectives' and too many 'red herrings'. A United States presidential speech writer once told me the ideal speech contains no more than three points and they should be repeated at least three times.

People are motivated largely by incentives. So, think about the people in your audience. What are their needs, wants and desires? If you have analysed your audience you should have no difficulty in choosing a subject. Think about the things they want to gain, what they want to be, what they want to do or what they want to save and you should be able to interest and motivate them.

What people want to *gain*
    Health
    Time
    Money
    Popularity
    Improved appearance
    Security in old age
    Praise from others
    Comfort
    Leisure
    Pride in accomplishment
    Business or social advancement
    Increased enjoyment
    Self-confidence
    Personal prestige.

What people want to *be*
    Good parents
    Sociable, hospitable
    Up to date
    Creative
    Proud of their possessions
    Influential over others
    Efficient
    'First' in things
    Recognised as authorities.

What people want to *do*
    Express their personalities
    Resist domination by others
    Satisfy their curiosity
    Emulate the admirable
    Appreciate beauty
    Acquire or collect things
    Win others' affection
    Improve themselves generally.

What people want to *save*

Time

Money

Work

Discomfort

Worry

Doubts

Risks

Personal embarrassment.

Get close to your audience

Before you start to prepare your next talk, do your homework. What sort of people are going to be your audience? How many do you expect? How much will they already know? What else do they need to know? What do they want to know? What are their worries and concerns?

People should be rewarded for making the effort to come to hear you. They want new information and new ideas and you can only provide that if you know what they don't know! Your first task is to find out who you will be speaking to and their knowledge gaps. Maybe they want reassuring but don't just tell them what they already know.

Your enthusiasm and sincerity can sway your audience if your message affects them personally. Don't be afraid to share your emotions and feelings – people like that. Try to reward them in some way, either emotionally by sharing a powerful story or by giving them useful information or the solution to an urgent problem.

Further information you will need

Make sure you have all the practical details about the meeting well in advance.

Find out when, where and at what time you are going to talk. Why were you invited? Who is chairing the meeting? How long are you expected to talk? Are you the only speaker? If not, what have the other speakers been asked to talk about? What other business has to be dealt with? What facilities are there for showing visual aids? Will there be questions from the audience and for how long?

When you know the answers to these questions you can start to think about the content of your talk. And finally, remember:

'In arranging your subject matter, you should keep in mind the fleeting nature of oral communication.'

◄ 11. ►

PLANNING YOUR SPEECH

You are ready to plan your speech when you have:

1. Decided on your subject
2. Studied your target audience
3. Learnt about your speaking environment.

Your first task is to decide on your objective.

What is your objective?

What is your aim, your objective? What message do you want to leave with your audience? What action do you want your audience to take after your speech? How are you going to get them to accept and act upon what you are going to tell them?

Are you going to inform, entertain, convince, persuade or inspire your audience?

Write down your message in one sentence.
(This is often the hardest part of preparing a speech.)

How to start planning your speech.

Outlining your speech

Let's call the sentence with your main message your *subject sentence*.

Next decide on the main points you want to discuss which support your subject sentence. Don't have too many of these – three or four is a good number. These are your main *supporting statements*. They are really minor summaries or arguments.

Take the first supporting statement, amplify it with data, examples, arguments or anecdotes. Then lead on smoothly to your next supporting statement, and so on.

Finally, summarise your main points into a strong memorable conclusion.

These first stages are illustrated in Figure 11.1 (over the page).

The formula for preparing a speech

1. *Analyse audience and environment*

2. *Write down*:

   - Purpose of your speech – your aim or objective; the response you want from your audience
   - Working title
   - Subject sentence (main message).

3. *Plan your draft outline* – main points and supporting statements.

Rules for preparing a speech summarised.

47

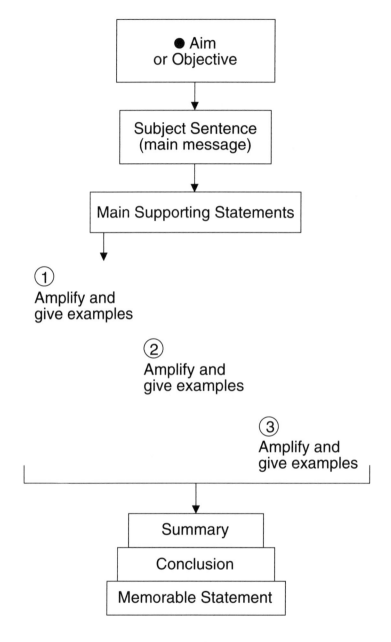

Figure 11.1 *Outlining your speech*

4. *Write speech* (a second version if it is to be published)

5. *Then write*:

   - Conclusion (review, make memorable statements)
   - Introduction (get attention and establish rapport)
   - Title (interesting, intriguing, explicit).

6. *Edit heavily*. Remove all unnecessary words and polish script until it sounds right.

7. *Prepare visual aids and handouts*

8. *Pick out key words*. Underline key words in script for headings for speech notes.

9. *Write headings on cards*.

Your planning checklist

The audience
Who are they?
How many are expected?
What are their worries, concerns and interests?

Their expectations
How much time has been allotted for my speech?
Will there be questions?
Do I need to prepare a handout?
Will reporters be present?

The environment
Where will I be speaking?
When?
Are there other speakers? (If so, what are they talking about?)
What other business is on the agenda?
Is there a lectern if I need one?
Will I need a microphone?
Are there facilities for visual aids? (Overhead projector, slide projector, screen, blackout curtains, display boards, laminated board, blackboard etc.)

Topic
My topic is . . .

Purpose
My purpose is to:

introduce
thank
support
inform
instruct
convince
inspire
motivate
get action
entertain.

Aim (objective)
My aim is . . . What response do I want?

Speech outline
What is your main message or *subject sentence*? Having clarified this, then organise your most important points and supporting statements:

- First point (main idea) leading to . . .
- Second point, leading to . . .
- Third point etc.

Conclusion
Summarise the main points.
Give a memorable message.
Call for action, if appropriate. (Make your appeal realistic.)

Now go back and write your introduction

Introduction
Get attention
Arouse interest

Reveal purpose of talk
Establish a rapport with audience.

Next decide on title

Title
Make it interesting or intriguing
Add an explicit sub-title (if necessary).

Now prepare your visual aids

Visual aids
What visual aids should I use to reinforce my message? (Remember they must be simple, understood and seen by all.) Examples are:

Overhead projector
Slide projector
Video
Film projector
Demonstrations
Boards (blackboard, laminated, magnet, flannel, chart)
Handouts
Models
The real thing.

'A speech should be ended, not allowed to expire. The end should be a climax, not an anti-climax.'
'A speech is like a love affair – any fool can start one, but to end it requires considerable skill.'

Lord Mancroft

SPEECH NOTES

Preparation

Never read an entire speech. Rehearse it thoroughly and makes notes from which you can speak.

There will be occasions when you will need to work from a written speech. While you are writing it, remember that the written word differs from the spoken word – we don't speak in formal sentences or paragraphs. We use groups or 'clusters' of words to convey our meanings. The fewer words in a sentence, the easier it is to understand. The fewer syllables in a word, the easier it is to understand. The more words about people, the more interesting your speech. The more statements addressed to your audience the more interesting it is to them.

With your outline as your guide, write out your speech in full. Don't worry about spelling, grammar or editing at this stage. Just let your ideas flow.

Read it through and change any parts you are not happy with.

Next, edit it heavily. Check on grammar and remove all surplus words.

Rehearsing your speech

Memorise your speech and record it. This will show what needs improvement.

A good technique for becoming thoroughly familiar with your subject matter is to record your speech. Exaggerate your vocal expression. Then listen carefully and alter anything to make it sound right. When you are satisfied play the recording twice a day for a week. You don't have to concentrate too hard on your talk; you can be doing other jobs at the same time. This is an easy way of learning a speech. Once you have the feeling and the rhythm of your speech you will find it easier to add topical comments or asides when you give your talk.

Nothing replaces thorough preparation. Memorise your speech so well that you seem to give it 'off the cuff'. You should only occasionally glance down at your notes. If you can use only key words or headings in your notes, so much the better.

No notes, only headings

To keep your audience interested, get rid of your notes and talk to them face to face. Take your written speech and use a marking pen to pick out key words. Underline just enough words to jog your memory and to keep you moving in your planned direction. Speak around these words – they become your headings. Keep them where you can glance at them from time to time to keep you on course.

Reduce the speech notes to headings.

If you are speaking without notes make sure you have a planned and polished introduction and conclusion. Learn them until you have them word perfect. A well-prepared introduction will help you to overcome any initial nervousness and a strong conclusion will leave your audience with your message ringing loud and clear.

How to make best use of speech notes

If you are presenting a formal paper or a policy statement, or if reporters are present, you will need speech notes. If your speech is to be printed you will need two versions, a paper for publication and notes for your oral presentation. Here are some useful guidelines for preparing speech notes.

A printed version for handing out is often essential at formal occasions.

- Use half sheets of paper – you are more likely to lose your place if you use full sheets. You can flip over half sheets easily and you can manage without a lectern. Don't staple them together but make sure you number them boldly.

- Type on one side of the paper only. Keep lines, sentences and paragraphs short.

- Avoid splitting a paragraph between two pages. Leave wide margins for last minute additions, corrections or topical ad libs.

- Make sure your notes are on thick paper that does not sag or rustle near a microphone. Yellow paper with black type is easy to read and helps you to find your speech notes quickly in a bag full of paper.

- Write as you would talk, in the language of your audience. Use personal pronouns. 'I believe you can make money by . . .' Use contractions. 'It's time we . . .' Use illustrative words, words with impact (for example devastated, slaughtered). Use words that arouse emotions (such as b-u-r-e-a-u-c-r-a-t-i-c).

- Don't use words you find difficult to pronounce. Watch out for technical words your audience may not fully understand. Use words to express, not impress.

- Hold your speech notes with your thumb in the margin. Keep your thumb opposite the line you are reading while you pause to ad lib or use a visual aid. This ensures that you do not lose your place.

Layout styles

Personal preferences play a part in how you set out your notes. Half sheets of paper have many advantages. Here are some layout styles to consider.

WHEN EVERYTHING IS IN CAPITALS, THERE IS NO EMPHASIS AND NOTHING JUMPS OUT OF THE PAGE. UNLESS THE SPEAKER HAS AN OUTSTANDING DELIVERY, THE RESULT IS A MONOTONE. A REAL DANGER IS THAT EMPHASIS WILL BE PLACED ON RELATIVELY UNIMPORTANT WORDS – OFTEN YOU'LL HEAR A SPEAKER STRESSING 'ANDS' AND 'BUTS'.

Speed is essential when scanning; you want instant recognition of groups of words, without losing your place. The following example is more helpful.

Your **eye** is not used to reading all capitals. Your newspapers and books are in **many small letters** (known as lower case) and few capitals.

Why not use capitals for EMPHASIS only, just as you would use <u>underlining</u>.

And for <u>EXTRA SPECIAL EMPHASIS</u> you could underline the capitals.

A good idea is to have the first few words of each paragraph underlined or in capitals. Project the first line to the left of the rest of the paragraph. This helps you to identify the paragraph more quickly. Some examples are given below.

<u>To set a climate for innovation we must challenge people</u>
> and remove frustrations.
> We must develop an environment
> that does not smother,
> but encourages, creative actions.

<u>Because we are so busy with day-to-day activities,</u>
> we tend to take our channels of
> communication for granted.
> To sit down and analyse objectively
> our sources of information,
> and the channels we use
> to get our messages to people,
> can be a revealing
> and rewarding exercise.

> **TYPED SPACE AND A HALF. HANGING SHOULDER LOWER CASE, UNDERLINED.**

<u>TO SET A CLIMATE FOR INNOVATION WE MUST CHALLENGE</u> PEOPLE
> and remove frustrations.
> We must develop an environment
> that does not <u>smother</u>,
> but <u>encourages</u>, creative actions.

BECAUSE WE ARE SO BUSY WITH DAY-TO-DAY
ACTIVITIES,

TYPED SPACE AND A HALF. HANGING SHOULDER CAPS. STRESS WORDS UNDERLINED. we tend to take our channels of communication for granted. To sit down and <u>analyse objectively</u> our sources of information, and the channels we use to get our messages to people, can be a <u>revealing</u> and <u>rewarding</u> exercise.

Some people find they can read more easily if they inset each new
line as has been done below.

<u>TO SET A CLIMATE FOR INNOVATION</u>
<u>WE MUST CHALLENGE PEOPLE</u>
and remove frustrations.
  We must develop an environment
  that does not smother,
    but encourages, creative actions.

<u>BECAUSE WE ARE SO BUSY</u>
<u>WITH DAY-TO-DAY ACTIVITIES,</u>
  we tend to take our channels of
  communication for granted.
    To sit down and analyse objectively
    our sources of information,
    and the channels we use
      to get our messages to people,
      can be a revealing and rewarding exercise.

TYPED SPACE AND A HALF. LEAD-IN CAPS UNDERLINED.

◀ 13. ▶

TIPS FROM PROFESSIONAL SPEAKERS

'A speech is like a journey – it has purpose, direction and an ultimate goal.'

What should you wear?

Dress for your audience. Try to mirror their dress. Your clothes should be comfortable and suit the occasion – but it's better to be overdressed than be dressed too casually.

Learn from the professionals.

First impressions

The way you begin your talk is very important. That's when you establish your credentials and build a rapport with your audience. A joke told against yourself or an appropriate anecdote helps. Try to relate to your audience at the start: 'I was born in this town and spent my schooldays here.'

A good start is very important.

When you get up to speak don't be in a hurry. Take time to compose yourself. Adjust the lectern, arrange your notes, adjust the microphone, take a deep breath, pause, look the audience over, then smile as at a friend.

'Mr Chairman, ladies and gentlemen . . .'

Share your feelings

Talk about your own experiences and describe your feelings.

Human emotions help to make a talk memorable.

Use good visual aids

A good visual aid can save you a lot of talking – but it must be simple and seen by all. A good visual aid can give you headings to talk to, serve as a memory jogger or show your audience what you are talking about.

Stick to the bare bones

Most inexperienced speakers try to cram in too much detail. Keep off sidetracks and 'red herrings'. Three or four well-chosen points are about right. Tell them what you are going to tell them. Make each point, illustrate and amplify it, then sum up with a memorable conclusion.

Watch your audience

To be convincing you must learn to keep eye contact with your audience. Watch them closely throughout your speech. How are they reacting to what you are saying? If they look puzzled, pause and explain what you mean. If they look bored, tell them a story. If they look weary, give them a break.

If you dry up

Don't panic if you suddenly lose your train of thought and 'dry up'. First of all, pause and compose yourself. Make it look a natural break. Then start off talking on another point, in another direction.

Be enthusiastic

An audience responds to an enthusiastic speaker – enthusiasm is contagious.

Don't drone on

Nothing is worse than a speaker who drones on in a monotone.

Excitement and enthusiasm will lift the interest level of a talk. Try varying the length of your sentences but better short than long.

Practise reading aloud

Practise reading aloud to strengthen your voice. Read extracts from books, poems, anything you enjoy. Reading to children is great practice. Try putting feelings and expression into your voice. Learn to say words and phrases precisely. By reading aloud with precision you will soon be able to obtain clarity at speed.

Check the sound system first

If you are using a microphone, test it before the meeting starts. You will need a higher sound level when the hall is full of people. Find out how to adjust the microphone height and whether there is an on/off switch.

Always talk across the microphone and never move away from it unless you are going to shout, cough or sneeze. If you are going to talk quietly and confidentially move close to the microphone.

If you are using a hand-held amplifier outside, place your back to the wind. Hold the microphone steady and plant your elbow firmly against your hip; as you move you will then be talking across the microphone.

Addressing the meeting

There has been much controversy over recent years about the way the person in authority at a meeting is addressed or referred to. Opinions vary from country to country and from organisation to organisation. Many accept the term 'chair' for the position of authority and the person is referred to as the 'chairman' or the 'chairperson'.

Always start your speech by addressing the chair. The preferred forms of address are 'Mister Chairman' or 'Madam Chair'. Avoid the term 'Madam Chairperson' or references to the 'chairwoman'.

It is acceptable to refer to the 'chairperson' but it is often easier to use the simple term 'the chair'.

During speeches or debates, comments and questions should always be addressed to the chair. Reference to other people is usually made in the third person: 'Madam Chair, the last speaker said she had not been informed . . .'

◀ 14. ▶

GUIDELINES FOR STORYTELLERS

To establish a rapport, tell a story. To explain a complicated issue, tell a story. To gain attention or to make your message memorable, tell a story. The poet Cowper gave us some useful guidelines:

> 'A tale should be judicious, clear, succinct,
> The language plain, the incidents well linked;
> Tell not as new what everybody knows;
> And, new or old, still hasten to a close.'

Everyone loves a story. Tell it well and you have their full attention.

Anecdotes are good

If you want to tell a story well, act it out. If you find acting difficult and cannot tell stories well, don't try. Keep to personal anecdotes based on your experiences – they are original and safer. Choose anecdotes which are appropriate for your audience and keep them brief. Your audience will 'warm' to you if you tell stories against yourself. For example:

> 'I made a great hit with my speech last night.'
> 'What did you talk about?'
> 'About five minutes.'

Humour

> 'A little nonsense now and then is relished by the wisest men.'

Humour is more important than jokes. Never tell jokes about a minority group unless you are a member of it.

The essence of humour is that it should be unexpected. It should contain an element of surprise. Humour is often emotional chaos remembered in tranquillity.

A good joke can lift a lecture. It can make a memorable point. You can spice up a talk with carefully selected and well presented jokes. Here are some hints to help you tell humorous stories.

- You must like the story to tell it well.

- Get yourself into the story. Make it *your* story.

- Tell stories against yourself. Play yourself down, others up.

- Try working up stories with groups of three statements.

  'My husband would not chase after other women – he's too loyal, too true (pause) – too old.'

- Practise your pausation to get your timing right – don't be in a hurry.

  'Behind every successful man you will find a good woman (pause) – and a surprised mother-in-law.'

- Keep your stories simple.

  'Recently a friend went to the doctor and was told she had only a few hours to live. "Is there anyone you would like to see?" the doctor asked. "Yes, another doctor."'

- Ridiculous situations are usually good for a laugh.

  'I was shocked to see my name in the death column of the local paper. I phoned and complained. The receptionist told me it was probably only a similarity of names. "No", I said. "You have my address right." After a lengthy pause she said, "Excuse me, where are you ringing from?"'

- Remember, 'A jest loses its point when he or she who makes it is the first to laugh.' Keep a straight face. Don't laugh at your own jokes.

Telling your story

When you hear a good story, jot it down. Rewrite it in your own words. Read it aloud. Edit it. Make it topical. Make it your story. Revise it, test it, rehearse it. Act it out using facial expressions and gestures in front of a mirror. Practise it on friends. Keep on telling it until you get it word perfect. File it so you can use it on the next appropriate occasion.

Tell a story in your own words, not someone else's. It sounds spontaneous that way.

15

MAKING YOUR LECTURES MEMORABLE

Show your audience how to get more from the lecture.

Lectures are an ineffective way to teach, particularly for teaching a skill. Always keep in mind the fleeting nature of oral communication. Introduce group participative techniques such as workshops, seminars, discussions, debates and role playing, as often as possible into your sessions. If there is no alternative but to lecture, you can become more effective if you follow the simple rules set out below.

1. Encourage note taking
Invite your audience to take notes. Ask them to record principles and ideas – not details. Details can be included in a handout you give out at the *end* of the lecture. Don't give it out at the beginning or you will have people reading instead of listening.

2. Use visual aids
Use visual aids as signposts or memory joggers. A good picture can be worth a thousand words. The more senses you can stimulate, the more memorable your message.

3. Illustrate your points
Use stories, anecdotes and figures of speech to illustrate your points. These can lift the interest level and make your lectures more memorable. A good story also serves as a memory jogger.

4. Use repetition

Introduce devices such as repetition to heighten drama. 'I had a dream the other night. I had a dream that you were there. I had a dream that we were rafting down this dangerous river . . .'

Use the 'three formula' – it can be a powerful oratory tool. Repeat certain key phrases three times to reinforce your message.

5. Limit your contents

Be careful not to cram too many points into a single lecture. Three points made three times is ideal. Distribute details or references to interested people when you have finished.

6. Use selective listening

Prepare your audience for selective listening. 'At the finish we will discuss [or test] . . . Be prepared to ask or answer questions on these aspects . . .'

7. Encourage questions

Invite questions from the audience. Use group techniques to prepare questions. 'Discuss my talk with the person sitting next to you for five minutes. Be prepared to ask a question.'

8. Review and summarise

An old teaching principle is, 'Tell them what you are going to tell them, tell it to them, then tell them what you have just told them.'

16

GUIDELINES FOR ANSWERING QUESTIONS

Guidelines

Taking questions from the floor.

- Ask the chairperson to repeat the question before you attempt to answer. This ensures that everyone in the audience has heard the question clearly. It also gives you time to think about your answer.

- Don't be afraid to restate or rephrase the question to clarify a point. You can always say, 'As I understand it, you are asking . . .' Turn obscure and pointless questions into intelligent ones, or ones you can answer. Start with the comment, 'A good question', then rephrase it.

- Always speak through the chair. Avoid conversing directly with the questioner – the exchange is for the benefit of the whole audience.

- Answer briefly. Keep your comments short and to the point.

- The chair should be impartial and take questions in order. If there is no chairperson, hold aggressive questioners by saying, 'Please wait a moment. The lady on the right was next.'

- Don't try to answer a question unless you know the answer. Your listeners will respect you more if you are honest with them. Don't be afraid to say, 'I cannot answer that question. I haven't got the details. I shall find out and let you know the answer next week. Come and see me.'

Answering interjections and hostile questions

If you have to deal with hostile audiences, there are certain principles you should observe.

Dealing with interrupters and hecklers.

- Make sure you have prepared your presentation well so you are confident about your subject matter – then you will not be taken by surprise with difficult questions.

- Deal with your topic in a professional, objective manner. Keep to the facts – don't make statements which can't be substantiated. Don't introduce personalities and don't introduce 'red herrings'.

- Speak in clear, concise English and avoid clichés and statements that have no clear meanings. Every sentence should contain something that makes the listener concentrate – preferably telling them something they did not know.

- Make your talk interesting. Gain and retain the audience's attention. If the audience is interested and does not lose concentration, there is little scope for interjections.

If you want to control your audience, you must be able to see their faces to get feedback, so make sure the auditorium is well lit. Monitor your audience constantly. If you want to perform well, you must have a good physical environment – a good introduction by the chairperson, a suitable podium, a good sound system and comfortable surroundings.

An experienced speaker can often play one sector of a hostile audience off against another. The technique can range from simply shouting them down to trapping them and leading them on. The speaker always has the advantage of being at a higher level on a stage and having a microphone.

Interjections

Dealing with interjections is a high risk activity. Unless you are a very experienced speaker, it is best to ignore interjections. Ignoring an interjector is frequently as devastating as an appropriate answer. Don't answer unless you can answer effectively.

Some speakers can say something humorously devastating with a quick one-liner. Others can answer an interjection by speaking briefly about the subject raised and then immediately moving on to a subject that will get the audience's attention. The audience will then have little patience if the interjector continues to interrupt.

Interjectors know that the art of interjection is to wait until the speaker pauses for breath then interject loudly, precisely and preferably humorously, when the speaker is at a disadvantage. An experienced speaker knows this and will often pause in unexpected places.

'Keep your cool.' Don't get angry under *any* circumstances and that's easier said than done!

Be polite and respectful even when confronted by a heckler trying to embarrass you. Audiences appreciate 'fair play' and respond to good manners. You can be curt and still be courteous. If you lose your temper you lose the argument.

Hostile questions
At the beginning, tell your audience you will try to answer any fair questions but you do not intend to answer 'loaded questions'.

The chairperson should deal with persistent questioners and interjectors. It is the chair's job to say, 'Our speaker has already answered several of your questions. It is only right that others are given a turn.'

If there are hostile groups with a grievance and they interject persistently, invite them to form a deputation to put their point of view to a subcommittee at a specific time and place.

When you have tried the above techniques and it is obvious you have an organised group setting out to break up your meeting, ask someone to telephone the police to get them evicted. Stop being charitable when a group is hostile and violent.

As John A Lee wrote, 'Be friendly until you are sure your interjector is an antagonist, then be intelligently pugnacious; later, if need be, reach for a verbal sledge-hammer; lastly get the police to evict.'

◄ 17. ►

CHANGING AUDIENCE ATTITUDES

First try to establish common ground with your listeners – establish a rapport. This can often be done by using one or more of the following.

- An anecdote or a story is always a good way to start. Use humour that is pertinent and in good taste, especially if it is at your own expense. Try telling a story against yourself.
- Show concern, understanding and friendliness towards your listeners. Before you start to talk, take time to compose yourself and make the effort to smile at friends in the audience.
- Refer to experiences which you hold in common with them.
- Quote or indicate your association with persons the audience regard highly.
- Tell them you agree with some of their hopes, beliefs, attitudes or values.

Always:
- Be polite and respectful.
- Be honest and straightforward; you won't change attitudes if you are not sincere.
- Be careful not to appear conceited or antagonistic.
- Show you have expertise and experience in the subject you are talking about.
- Try to be fair, flexible, modest and good natured.
- Dress appropriately for the occasion. (If you are in doubt, it is better to be overdressed than too casual.)

Get the audience on your side by reminding them what you have in common.

◄ 18. ►

INTRODUCING A SPEAKER

How much time?

When you are chairing a meeting with a guest speaker, it is your job to introduce the speaker. Just before the introduction, make sure the speaker knows how much time is allocated for the talk. 'It's now nine o'clock. We will take questions at twenty past nine and finish at nine thirty sharp!'

A good introduction raises audience expectations and gets the speaker off to a flying start.

Introduce the speaker

Stand and tell the audience briefly what the subject is and why the speaker has been chosen to talk about it. It is your job to 'sell' the speaker to the audience. First, you must get your listeners interested so they will direct their attention to the speaker and the topic. You must promote the speaker and the subject. As well as introducing the speaker to the audience you must introduce the audience to the speaker. 'In this club we have the leading bankers in town and they are always looking for new ideas.' This creates an atmosphere that makes the audience more receptive and allows the speaker to perform well.

Mention qualifications and experience

Mention the speaker's qualifications and experience and the speaker's title or position. Don't give a complete biography – just the parts pertinent to the speech or things that reinforce the authenticity of the subject matter. Tell the audience if there will be time for questions at the end of the talk. Give the speaker's name as the final word of your introduction.

Lead the applause

Keep looking at the speaker and continue the applause until the speaker is ready to begin.

◀ 19. ▶

THANKING A SPEAKER

Vote of thanks

In your vote of thanks, mention points raised by the speaker to show you were deeply interested.

When a guest speaker has addressed a meeting, it is usual for the audience to show their appreciation formally by passing or 'moving' a vote of thanks. This is a special type of motion, so all remarks should be addressed to the chair.

Warn the mover

Before the speech, the chair should notify the person who will be asked to move the vote of thanks. The mover is then prepared and if necessary can make notes during the address. At the end of the speech the mover rises – usually after a nod from the chair.

Speak for the audience

'Madam Chair, I have much pleasure in moving a vote of thanks to Mr Ross for his fine address tonight . . .'

Show a lively appreciation of what was said. Comment on a few points of interest in the speech and the manner of presentation. Show that you genuinely enjoyed the speech – try to speak for the whole audience. Be brief, be witty. Thank the speaker sincerely and modestly. Do not criticise the subject matter even if you disagree with it.

'I wish to move a sincere vote of thanks to Mr Ross . . .'

It is not necessary to have a seconder for this motion.

Carried by acclamation
The chair puts the motion to the audience and it is usually carried
by acclamation (clapping). The meeting (not the mover) 'passes' the
vote of thanks.

◀ 20. ▶

GUIDELINES FOR USING VISUAL AIDS

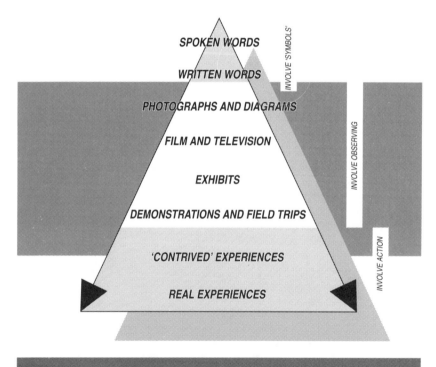

Figure 20.1 *The value of various aids to learning*

If we study the learning process we find that words alone are very ineffective as a means of teaching. However, by combining them with visual aids such as photographs, diagrams, films, videos, models and demonstrations you can improve the effectiveness of your speeches and lectures. Use visual aids at every appropriate opportunity – they will add interest and variety to your presentations. Figure 20.1 illustrates this.

Visual aids reinforce the verbal message and help listeners to retain it

There are three golden rules for visual aids. They must be:

- Simple
- Understood
- Seen by all.

Choosing the appropriate visual aids

The visual aids you choose will depend on the type of information you want to present, the size of the audience and the venue. Your venue could be a small room, a large auditorium or the 'great outdoors'. They will also depend on the equipment and assistance available and whether it is possible to black out the room or hall.

Make sure the visual aids you choose are the best ones to illustrate your points. They must be the most suitable for the size of your audience and for your venue. Table 20.1 lists the various types and the appropriate uses.

Table 20.1 *Visual aids and their uses*

| Visual aid | Audience size | | | | Needs dark room | Needs power plug |
	50	100	200	1,000		
Actual object	*	*	*	*	No	*
Blackboard	Yes	No	No	No	No	No
Chart and display board	*	*	*	No	No	No
Comic strip and cartoon	*	No	No	No	No	No
Film	Yes	Yes	Yes	Yes	Yes	Yes
Flannelboard	Yes	No	No	No	No	No
Magnetboard	Yes	No	No	No	No	No
Model	Yes	*	*	No	No	*
Overhead projector	Yes	Yes	Yes	Yes	No	Yes
Paper pad	Yes	No	No	No	No	No
Poster	*	No	No	No	No	No
Slide (35 mm)	Yes	Yes	Yes	Yes	Yes	Yes
Videotape and closed-circuit television	Yes	*	No	No	Yes	Yes
'You'	Yes	Yes	Yes	Yes	No	No

*Depends on circumstances

Always try to demonstrate with the real thing, if possible. It will be far more effective than any substitute. Also, an 'active' visual aid such as a film or a working model will be more effective than anything passive such as a chart or a table of figures. The mere act of writing on a transparency or of rearranging the objects on a magnetboard will arouse more interest than a completely static, prepared chart or diagram.

Your choice of visual aid will depend on:

- The information you are trying to convey
- The equipment that is available
- Which you like best
- What help you can call on in preparing your visual aids
- Whether a black out is possible
- The size of your audience
- Where you are speaking.

Always practise beforehand, with all your equipment set up, in the room where you will be speaking. If you plan to use a slide projector or show films, be sure to have a spare bulb and a screwdriver (or, better still, a spare projector) handy. When you have set up your projector (or any other aid) move about the room to see if there are any 'blind' spots. Remember, the older your audience, the bigger, brighter and clearer your picture needs to be. If you are using a visual aid *everyone* must be able to see it clearly.

Rules for using slides and transparencies

Slides and transparencies should be simple, easily understood and visible from the back of the room.

- *One idea only.* Limit the amount of information on a transparency or slide to a single idea. Don't make several points on one visual aid.

- *Use title phrases.* Use clear simple title phrases so the audience knows immediately what the visual is about; for example 'Gross Income' *not* 'Chart No 1'.

- *Must be seen by all.* Make sure all visual aids can be seen clearly from the back and the corners of a room. Use the six/six rule – no more than six lines on a slide or transparency and six words per line.

- *Rehearse.* Have a rehearsal in the room you will be using. Anticipate problems. Check power points to see if they are live.

Know the position of the switches. Check black-out facilities. Check the height and angle of the screen, so that the whole audience can see it with no heads in the way. If you are using an overhead projector, angle the screen. Make sure you have a spare bulb or that there is another projector available in case of emergency.

- *Coordinate your talk and visual aids.* Show a visual aid only when you are talking about that topic.

- *Allow time.* Give your audience time to study each 'visual' and allow yourself time to explain details, if necessary.

- *Switch off.* Keep your 'visual' on the screen while the projector is turned on – don't blind your audience with white light. When you want to direct attention back to yourself, cover up the 'visual' or turn the projector off.

- *Watch your audience.* Talk to your audience *not* to your 'visual'. Watch your audience to see if they are understanding your visual aid.

- *Not too many.* Don't overdo visual aids. Use a a few good ones; too many are boring.

- *Handouts.* If people want additional information or details, give them handouts *after* you have finished talking.

◀ 21. ▶

THE VARIETIES OF VISUAL AIDS

How to choose the most appropriate visual aid.

There are many types of visual aid but sometimes the simplest ones are the most effective. This section lists some of the common visual aids with their advantages and disadvantages and practical hints on using them. The types covered are:

Blackboard and laminated board
Chart and display board
Comic strip and cartoon
Film
Flannelboard
Magnetboard
Model
Overhead transparency
Paper pad
Poster
35 mm slide
Videotape and closed-circuit television.

Blackboard and laminated board

Advantages
- Low cost
- Allows use of colour
- Suitable for compiling lists
- Good for 'building up' a story

- Good for illustrating a point during question time
- An 'active' visual, that is it involves movement with the speaker writing or drawing, this arouses interest and adds variety to the talk.

Disadvantages

- Chalk is dusty and the expensive pens for laminated boards tend to leak or dry up
- You turn your back on your audience when you are writing – unless you prepare your board beforehand
- You should clean or remove the board before you move on to next point
- Speakers often stand between their audience and the board
- Unsuitable for a large audience because of its limited visibility
- You need practice in drawing and printing clearly to use it well.

Tips

- Before you use a new blackboard, fill its pores with chalk dust by patting the entire surface with a chalked duster – this prevents permanent impressions.

- Don't stand in front of the board and remember (as with other visual aids), practice improves performance.

- Prepare complicated diagrams before you start. Cover them and expose them when they are required.

- If possible don't try to do complicated diagrams in front of your audience. If you must do so, use templates or a pencil to draw guidelines before you talk.

- Laminated boards are ideal for small meetings. They are not dusty like blackboards and many can also be used as magnetboards.

Chart and display board

Advantages

- Gives a brief visual message

- Good for summarising points
- Can be prepared by a signwriter, using good layout and colour.

Disadvantages

- Often large and awkward to carry
- Not suitable for large audiences
- Must be removed before you go on to the next point in your talk or it is a distraction.

Tips

- Signwriters' calico is ideal for a portable chart, and poster paints are suitable for the lettering.

- For an audience of 40, a chart should be at least 55 by 70 cm.

- Most people can see 3 cm-high lettering from 10 m.

- Use no more than six or seven lines on a chart.

- Lettering must be thick. Exaggerate the spacing between letters and words.

- Your chart can be made into a 'striptease' chart if you use thick paper or light card to cover the text or drawings. (Adhesive tape wound sticky side outward around two fingers held slightly apart, gives a two-sided sticky surface to hold up the cover sheet.) Then you can expose your message gradually.

Comic strip and cartoon

Don't overlook the comic strip and the cartoon when you want to get a message across. Both of them, if used effectively, will attract attention and arouse interest. Their success depends on the ability and the imagination of the creator.

The comic strip aims to entertain by telling a story in a series of drawings. The story should be brief and packed with action. It should deal with an exciting or an amusing situation. Scripts should be brief and simple.

A well-designed comic strip can be a useful educational handout. Bright colour can make it more effective.

The serious cartoon is often intended to influence public opinion by caricaturing a person, an idea, or a situation. The humorous cartoon is usually intended to amuse but can be used to convey a very serious message.

Advantages
- Almost universal appeal (most people are lazy readers but eager lookers)
- Can attract both the literate and the illiterate
- A clever cartoon or comic strip will sometimes be published free by a newspaper, as a community service.

Disadvantages
- A clever scriptwriter and artist are needed
- The artist needs to fully understand the local scene and sense of humour.

Tips
A good cartoon:

- Deals with a single idea
- Simplifies issues
- Is well drawn
- Has humour
- Usually has only a brief caption
- Can be readily understood by the 'target' audience.

Film

Advantages
- Excellent for showing action and for demonstrating
- Can condense or 'stretch' time
- Good for close-up demonstrations

- Suitable for large audiences
- Can reproduce the past for today's lessons.

Disadvantages
- Expensive to produce
- Projectors are usually heavy and expensive
- Some skill is required to set up and operate a projector
- The film producer takes control of your meeting.

Tips
- A verbal introduction is helpful.

- Use your film (or part of it) to help illustrate a point – don't let the film take over completely.

- After a film involve your audience. Use the screening as a means to stimulate worthwhile discussions. Ask questions: 'Did you agree with . . .? What did you like best about . . .? What were the main points?'

Flannelboard

Advantages
- Cheap to make
- Can be rolled up
- An 'active' visual (*see* blackboard).

Disadvantages
- Not suitable for large audiences
- Not as reliable as a magnetboard
- Not suitable for outdoor use.

Tips
- Any rough-textured cloth such as flannel or blanket can be used. Pin it tightly and securely on a solid backing. (You can attach it to a blackboard with spring clips.)

- The flannel should be a neutral colour.

- Graphics should be prepared on stiff, light cardboard with sandpaper or rough-textured cloth stapled or glued lightly to the back. (Too much glue can mat the fibres and prevent the graphics sticking to the flannelboard.)

- For heavy graphics or for outdoor demonstrations in windy conditions, use Velcro (two materials, one covered with hooks and the other with loops, which cling together).

- Write the name on the back of each piece. This saves time when assembling the whole show.

- Make sure your board is tilted slightly backwards or your graphics may fall off.

Magnetboard

Advantages
- Any iron or steel surface (such as a steel cabinet) can be used
- Suitable for outdoor use
- Good for television visuals if surface is dull
- An 'active' visual.

Disadvantages
- Heavy to transport
- Graphics with magnets attached are time consuming to prepare.

Tips
- Magnets can be either small pot, bar, or flexible plastic tape (containing embedded magnetic filings).

- Attach the magnetic strip to light card with glue, adhesive tape or staples.

- A metal-gauze screen makes a lightweight magnetboard, but needs a rigid frame. A picture, map or drawing can be mounted behind the screen for greater effect.

- Bottle tops make good 'players' for showing sports-team movements on a magnetboard. Glue 2 cm pieces of plastic-strip magnet inside bottle tops which have been painted and numbered appropriately.

Model

There are several types of model:

- *scale models*, smaller or bigger than the original but in correct proportions
- *cutaway models*, where pieces can be removed to reveal what is inside
- *build-up models*, where pieces can be added to complete a model
- *working models*, powered by a person, batteries, electricity, animals etc.

Advantages

- Shows principles or characteristics when you cannot use the real thing
- Can be smaller or bigger than the real thing; can also be simpler
- Easy for most people to understand
- Gets attention and fascinates some people especially if it is a working model.

Disadvantages

- Often expensive to make
- Often difficult to pack and transport
- Rarely suitable for large audiences.

Tips

- It must be large enough and simple enough for everyone in the audience to see and understand.

- It must be accurate enough to be convincing.

- It should be strong and easily portable. Make sure you have good containers for transporting.

- A working model must be easy to operate and maintain.

- Remember a model is usually a poor substitute for the real thing. If possible, demonstrate with the real thing.

Overhead transparency

Advantages
- Can be used in a lighted room
- You can maintain eye contact with your audience – you can write or draw as you talk
- 'Active' (like a blackboard)
- Suitable for small or large audiences
- Transparency can be prepared earlier and by exposing a little at a time, you can build up a story.

Figure 21.1 (over the page) illustrates some of these advantages.

Disadvantages
- Requires some operating skills
- Screen should be angled 90 degrees from the projector's lens
- Lamp is fragile
- Can be bulky to transport
- Heat from the lamp and the bright light can cause discomfort
- If your writing or drawings are untidy, this will be accentuated on the screen.

Tips
- Ideally don't have more than six lines of writing on a transparency or more than six words per line.

- Keep the lettering at least 6 mm high.

- Most photocopying machines can be used to produce overhead transparencies but you must use plain paper-copier transparency film.

- Photocopying machines that enlarge can be used to make transparencies from text, cartoons or drawings in publications.

- You may have to enlarge several times to get the correct size.

- If you clip and paste to make a visual you will find a glue stick handy. You will not need to cover the edges of additions with white paint to stop them showing on the transparency if you reduce the contrast on the photocopier.

1. Print your own visuals while you talk.

2. Use a sheet of paper or card to expose your message progressively.

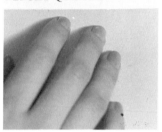

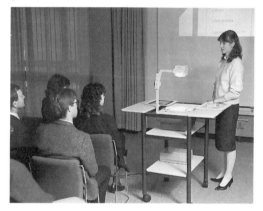

3. Use a pen or pencil as a 'Pointer'.

4. Use overlays in contrasting colours to build up your story.

Figure 21.1 *The advantages of an overhead projector*

- Some desktop publishing computers have graphics packages which enable you to make transparencies.

Paper pad (large sheets of plain paper) or flip charts

Advantages
- Readily available
- Low cost
- Easy to carry (roll them up)
- Easy to prepare using large coloured crayons or thick felt pens
- Can be prepared beforehand
- You can 'ghost write' details in pencil
- As each sheet is finished, it is turned over so it does not remain as a distraction
- It is easy to refer back to previous sheets
- You can mask sections and strip off covers at appropriate times to reveal message
- Sheets can sometimes be used again
- Sheets can be torn off and stuck to a wall with masking tape to build up a plan. Some are pre-glued for this purpose.

Disadvantages
- Suitable only for small audiences
- Needs some type of easel support
- The speaker turns away from audience to write on the pad or read from it
- Some speakers stand in front of it
- Unsuitable for outdoor use.

Tips
- Thick crayons are more reliable than felt pens.
- You can pin the pad to your lectern with drawing pins. Drape the sheet with your visual aid in front of the lectern. You can have any notes you require written on the back of the next sheet. Drop that sheet over the lectern at the appropriate time to expose the next visual.
- Opaque white plastic is more durable than paper and can be used instead.

Poster

A poster is useful for getting a single important idea across quickly. It should have strong eye appeal to attract attention.

Advantages
- Can be displayed for its artistic value as well as for its message
- Can remain on display for lengthy periods
- Can be transported easily and cheaply
- Can be produced cheaply by silk screening or colour photocopying.

Disadvantages
- Often costly to design
- A big print run is needed to make glossy posters economic
- Must be displayed where people have time to look at it.

Tips
A good poster has:

- A simple message
- Bold design
- Bright colours
- Brief, clear wording.

35 mm slide

Advantages
- Projectors are readily available at most venues
- Slides are easy to carry and store
- Slides are easy to duplicate
- Slides can be rearranged and others added to keep a series topical
- Very small objects can be enlarged on a screen
- Objects are shown in natural colour

- Speaker controls the speed so can explain or answer questions if necessary
- Suitable for large or small audiences.

Disadvantages
- Time-consuming to prepare and process
- If you have a projectionist, you must coordinate and practise your presentation
- Needs black-out facilities
- Speaker loses eye contact with audience during blackout
- Rapid light changes are distracting.

Tips
- Aim for one idea per slide

- Keep wording to a minimum.

- Add colour to a black and white slide by backing it with a coloured blank (in the same mount) or by painting it with food-colouring dye.

- Typescript is too small for 35 mm slides but in an emergency you can make a slide quickly by cutting a stencil on a manual typewriter. Keep within the 23 mm by 34 mm of the mounted slide (up to four lines of 14 characters). Trim your typed script and fix into a slide mount.

- Sort and label all your slides and arrange them in containers or carousels in logical order.

- Put a thumb spot on the lower left-hand corner of each slide. Slides are inserted in the projector upside down with the thumb spot at the right-hand corner.

- Arrange the room and seating and check all equipment before your presentation.

- Have a test run to make sure the slides are in the correct order and none is upside down or back to front.

- When you set up your projector, always wrap the lead around the leg of the table it is placed on. Then if someone trips over the lead in the dark, the projector won't crash to the floor. Tape the lead to the floor for extra safety.

- Check that light from your lectern does not fall on the screen.
- Face your audience when you talk – not the screen!
- Don't leave a slide on for a long time. Most people will grasp important points in 15 seconds.
- If you want to talk between slides, slip in a blank, pleasantly coloured slide (easily made by photographing the sky or a coloured card).
- Use a remote control attachment and set your own pace.
- A projector can be used as an emergency spotlight to illuminate a speaker or a display.
- If you have to show slides to a small group in daylight you can make an emergency rear-projection screen from a cardboard box and greaseproof paper (not waxed paper).

How many slides will you show?

This will depend on the nature of your talk and whether you are talking about the slides or using them only to illustrate certain points. *But don't use too many.*

- For a 20-minute talk, ten slides are often adequate.
- Show only the best – leave out the rest.

| 10 slides | 20 slides | 40 slides |

Videotape and closed-circuit television

Modern video cameras – 'camcorders' – are very portable, easy to operate and enable you to play colour videos almost instantly. Videotapes for educational purposes should be well planned and rehearsed, and produced by skilled camera and sound technicians.

Advantages
- 'Captures' an event so it can be replayed later, often at a more convenient time
- Instant replay is possible
- Can be replayed many times and stopped for discussions
- Can show close-ups to a large audience
- Can be used to magnify very small objects
- Shows objects in natural colour
- Graphics, film clips and slides can be inserted where appropriate
- Outdated material can be edited out
- People can watch themselves and evaluate their own performances.

Disadvantages
- Equipment is costly at present – particularly large screen projectors
- Television sets for viewing are not readily portable
- Support equipment needs to be compatible
- Detailed planning is often necessary
- Extra lighting is usually needed
- Skilled camera and sound technicians and studio facilities are needed for quality productions
- Production can be time consuming and costly
- People are often critical of amateur productions because they are familiar with highly professional standards in cinemas and commercial television.

Tips
- See section on television (pages 101–104).

- When using graphics don't use white card – black lettering on grey or light blue is best.

- Make graphics one-third wider than their height. Be careful edges are not masked when reproduced on screen.

- Have no more than four or five lines of printing on each visual and try not to use more than 15 letters or spaces per line.

◄ 22. ►

BE YOUR OWN VISUAL AID

- An effective speech comes from the heart, with emotions, movements and some acting.

- The way you dress, the way you move, the way you sound can each do a lot of 'talking' for you.

- Most of the impact you make will be non-verbal – through your facial expressions, your tone of voice and your movements and gestures.

- Use your hands to illustrate movement and form. The volume, speed and tone of your voice should reflect your emotions.

- You will catch and maintain attention if you pause occasionally. Slow down your delivery. Speak distinctly, but without strain. Try to develop a rapport with your audience.

- Dress appropriately – avoid flamboyant clothes that may distract your audience.

- Move naturally and confidently – avoid any annoying mannerisms. Ask your friends to point these out to you, so you can make an effort to overcome them.

- Make an effort to be enthusiastic always – enthusiasm is contagious.

- Mime is a very effective, non-verbal form of communication. A shrug of the shoulders, a smile, a look of dejection can say more than words.

The speaker's appearance and manner can send visual signals to the audience. Make sure you are sending the right ones.

- Television's 'close-up' allows you to make full use of facial expressions and gestures. Remember, however, movements and expressions are exaggerated in close-up, so be natural and don't overemphasise.

Read *Effective Presentation Skills* by Steve Mandel (Kogan Page).

◀ 23. ▶

BROADCASTING YOUR MESSAGES

Radio

**Radio can reach
people everywhere.
It makes demands on
their imagination.**

Radio is the best medium for getting your message to a wide
audience quickly. It has a sense of immediacy but its strength lies in
its intimacy. It should be like a one-to-one conversation. So when
you are speaking on radio, visualise friends and pretend you are
chatting to them.

Publicising your cause

If you want to publicise your cause through radio news:

- Pick a time when there is little other news.
- Be different. Make your story newsworthy. Be controversial, make predictions, arouse interest, say something unusual.
- If possible, arrange an early interview with a radio journalist. Explain why your cause is interesting and should be broadcast.

Being interviewed

- If you are to be interviewed plan what you want to say, particularly the final message – the one you want your audience to remember.

- Keep your answers concise and to the point. Keep hammering the points you wish to make from different angles.

- The interviewer's job is to ask questions for the listeners, so prepare answers for possible difficult questions.

- Don't worry about your voice levels – the technician or broadcaster can adjust the position of the microphone and the controls to suit your voice. But once voice levels are set don't push your chair back away from the microphone.

- Use your hands, make gestures and chat informally to your interviewer.

- Keep one eye on the clock and make your main summary point last.

- A recorded radio talk is easy to edit or redo. If you flounder or stumble or are not happy with what you said, say, 'Sorry, let's have another go at that question.'

When a reporter phones for a broadcast comment

When a reporter wants an answer immediately to a difficult question, make an excuse, any excuse. Say, 'Phone back in five minutes'. Use that time to prepare yourself, collect your thoughts, assemble your data, maybe consult a colleague and have your answer ready when the phone rings. Don't be rushed into making statements you may regret later.

Writing a radio script

You must write as if you were talking. Write 'talk-stuff' not 'book-stuff'. Writing a radio script is completely different from writing an article. In writing a talk, you can scrap most of what you've been taught on how to write. You've been told that it's bad to end a sentence with a preposition. It may be in print, but not in talk. To write as you would talk, you must talk as you write.

Listeners, unlike readers, can't go back to refresh their memories. So say what you are going to say, say it, and say what you have said. A good talk is like a good poem. It's not so much the argument – it's the impact.

A good script is one written in simple, direct sentences in the active voice. Words should be short, and technical terms avoided. The fewer words per sentence and the fewer syllables per word, the easier your script will be to read, and the easier for your listeners to understand. Talk directly to your audience in groups of words . . . like that . . . and then pause for your audience to take in each group. Use contractions as in conversation. Try to put excitement into your script. Write for hearing. Your script must sound right to the ear, like music.

Develop your topic logically – step by step. Start with an anecdote or something that the listener can relate to, then move on to something new. Concentrate on one or two important points, then repeat them at the end of your talk by way of a summary. Don't try to cover the whole field – concentrate on one aspect of your topic.

Guidelines for writing a radio script
- Write your script in the active voice.
- Use the present tense whenever possible.
- Use contractions as in conversation – 'it's', 'you'll', 'we've', 'don't'.
- Use phonetic spelling of names.
- Include anecdotes and examples from your own experience.
- Translate figures into comparisons. Any figures still in the script should be spelt out and rounded off, for example 'The city has a population of five million.'
- Use verbs freely – they're the driving force of a talk.
- Use link words and phrases to help the script flow – 'anyway', 'well', 'now', 'besides', 'but', 'on the other hand'.

- Use plenty of punctuation – dashes, commas and full stops.
- Type the script in double spacing. The final draft should be on heavy, half sheets of paper.
- Put in long dashes or oblique strokes to indicate pauses. Underline words that need emphasis (or type them in capitals).

Tips
- Never talk down to listeners
- Never offend anybody on an ethical or religious point
- Avoid bad language, vulgarisms
- Don't date a talk – don't refer to 'yesterday', 'last week'
- Don't use rhetorical questions
- Keep the sentence construction simple – avoid using dependent clauses
- Don't abbreviate names and titles unless you are sure everyone knows what you mean
- Avoid double negatives. Always go for the positive
- Avoid tongue twisters or multisyllabic words such as 'ineradicable'
- Avoid, as much as possible, long and abstract nouns ending in ' . . . ation', ' . . . ition'
- Avoid sibilants, such as 'such necessary sequences'
- Avoid alliteration and vowel sound clashes
- Avoid clichés
- Never use 'eg', 'ie' and 'etc' but write in link phrases 'such as', 'that is', 'and so on'.

A good script should:
- Aim at a specific response from the audience
- Catch attention at the start
- Keep to three or four main points
- Be logical
- Be simple, clear and brief
- Be personal and conversational
- Have illustrations from your own experiences
- Summarise the main points
- Say where to get further information.

Delivering your talk
Once you have written your script in your own words, read it aloud

to make sure it flows smoothly and there are no awkward passages. Practise delivering it as if you were talking to a friend. Try putting some excitement into it – mark pauses, words needing emphasis and changes of speed on your script. Don't rehearse it too much or it will lose spontaneity but know the script well enough to know what group of words comes next.

Before you start recording, relax and take a few 'abdominal' breaths. Relax your lower jaw and do a few mouth exercises, so you are prepared to open it well and articulate your words clearly. If you get nervous and get a very dry mouth or you have excess saliva, try licking a lemon or an apple. It also helps if you moisten your bottom lip just before going on air. Smile and remember to speak as if you are talking to a friend.

Start as soon as the red light comes on in the studio. Pitch your voice a little lower than normal and start off speaking slowly and clearly while your listeners are getting used to your voice. When on air, breathe through your mouth.

Television

Entertainment is vital
The essence of television is entertainment. If a programme lacks that vital strand of drama, human interest, humour or tragedy, you won't get air time.

Television demands less of the viewer than radio does of the listener. Make sure you grab and keep their attention.

Make your stories visual
Television has an insatiable appetite for visual material. Television staff are constantly on the lookout for stories with good visual impact, preferably with plenty of action. If you want publicity for your cause think up ways of making your message visual.

Use real people
Reporters want to film real people and real happenings, not a spokesperson for your cause.

Go for the live interview
If you have a choice always go for the live interview rather than the prerecorded interview. A live interview goes on air as you speak. It cannot be edited. But a prerecorded video film can be cut and edited down to a brief clip and is often used out of context. Often an opponent is asked to comment on selected statements and this puts you at a great disadvantage.

Handling mixed media interviews
What do you do if you are involved in a controversial meeting and walk out to face a battery of reporters?

Deal with newspaper and radio reporters first. Walk out of range of the television cameras and come back for a separate interview later.

Not behind your desk!
When a camera team comes to your office, don't let them interview

you behind your desk. Set out some easy chairs and a coffee table or stand in front of an appropriate backdrop.

Watch what you say
Some reporters deliberately let interviews go on for a long time in the hope that you will let your guard down and say something controversial or colourful. Be careful what you say. Remember the reporter is simply trying to make interesting and lively television for viewers.

Take time to answer.
Take time to think when asked a difficult question. Pauses can be edited out in a prerecorded interview. You can always blow your nose if you want time to think – that's always edited out.

Don't make excuses
Give honest direct answers – don't make excuses. 'No comment' is usually interpreted as 'You are right, but I am not prepared to confirm it'.

Guidelines for television interviews
- Wear lightweight clothes (for the heat in the studio). Avoid bold stripes, checks and jazzy patterns. A pastel-coloured shirt or blouse looks better than a white one.

- Don't drink alcohol before an interview – your viewers will be able to tell.

- Don't slump. Sit up straight in your chair.

- Look at your interviewer. Don't look at the floor or ceiling for inspiration.

- Don't call one another by name.

- Try for a strong start. If possible lead in with a punchy statement.

- Show enthusiasm – if necessary get excited. Try to be more animated than usual. Be interested in what you say and you'll sound interesting.

- Speak with confidence and authority. Talk conversationally, but convincingly and persuasively. Be credible.

- Be yourself; be as natural as possible. Don't answer in an official manner. You will irritate your viewers if you sound like a bureaucrat. Try to be sincere and informal.

- Speak in 'thoughts' – in groups of words, not in sentences. ('Talk stuff' not 'book stuff'.)

- Use 'person-to-person' psychology. Bring your viewers into your confidence.

- Smile only when appropriate, otherwise your viewers will get the wrong message and not trust you.

- The interviewer's job is to get you to answer the questions that are in the minds of viewers. Try to answer each question briefly and honestly. An interviewer applies pressure if you evade questions.

- Your job is to present facts, and to add to (or interpret) information. If you are discussing topical or controversial issues, you may have to correct misapprehensions. Correct your interviewer if you are being misrepresented.

- Keep control of the interview – don't lose your 'cool' under any circumstances. Try to retain your sense of humour even when you are provoked.

- Avoid speech mannerisms, especially jargon or clichés, such as 'at this point in time . . .', 'but first I would like to say . . .' and 'I think . . .'

- Your viewers will remember the way you react and the overall impression you make, rather than what you say.

◀ 24. ▶

TIPS FOR TELEPHONING

Making better use of your telephone

'The telephone is the greatest nuisance among conveniences, the greatest convenience among nuisances.'

The telephone is an essential part of business but most people have not been trained to use it effectively. When conducting business by telephone, perceptive listening becomes very important. Impressions depend entirely on what is heard. Your business calls should be planned and not be impromptu performances.

By putting the ideas in this section into practice you should improve your relationships with your clients and friends and increase your business.

The telephone call is often the first contact with a business. It must be well handled.

Involve your switchboard operator

Switchboard operators are usually the first contacts people have with your organisation, so they are very important people. Train them well. Keep them informed of staff responsibilities, dates, times and places of meetings, names of publications and activities of the office or department. The more you involve them the easier they will make your job.

Keep the operator informed of your movements

If the switchboard operator cannot find you when an important long-distance call comes through, it can be costly, frustrating and bad for business.

Make a list of telephone numbers you use often
To save time keep a list of frequently called numbers in an easily accessible form handy to your telephone.

Plan your calls
Before you place a call, list the points you want to cover or questions you want to ask.

Collecting information
When collecting information:

1. Identify yourself
2. Establish rapport
3. State the purpose of your call
4. Thank your informant politely.

Identify yourself confidently. If possible call the person by name:

> 'Good morning, Mr Ross. This is Robin Jay. I am the personnel manager of the Triple Z Computer Company.'

Establish rapport and state the purpose of your call – get to the point:

> 'Your friend Bill Thompson suggested I should telephone you. I need your help and advice, if you can spare a minute. We have an application from Cyril Jones for a job. He said he was one of your staff. Can you recommend him?'

Listen carefully, making notes if necessary. Thank your informant politely:

> 'I greatly appreciate your advice. I will treat it confidentially. If I can help you at any time please let me know. Thank you, Mr Ross.'

Selling

When wanting to sell something:

1. Identify yourself
2. Establish rapport
3. State and dramatise the purpose of your call
4. Arrange a personal visit or a demonstration
5. Conclude on a friendly note.

Identify yourself and your organisation:

'Good morning, Mr Ross. This is Robin Jay from the Triple Z Computer Company.'

Establish rapport:

'At last week's Lions' Club meeting, your golfing partner, Bill Brown, told me you were interested in buying a personal computer.'

State and dramatise the purpose of your call:

'I am calling you because we have just received a revolutionary personal computer at a very low price.'

Arrange a personal visit or a demonstration:

'Can I give you a demonstration at a time and place to suit you?'

Conclude on a friendly note:

'Thank you, Mr Ross, for giving me your time. I am looking forward to our meeting in your office next Wednesday the 10th at 11 am.'

Use names

If possible, call the person you contact by name. If you are not sure of the name and position of the person you want to talk to, check this out first with the telephone operator at their office. If you cannot get past a protective secretary who demands to know your business, try bluffing the operator with a fictitious name; so as to get the real one:

'I would like to speak to your General Manager, Mr John Jones please.' 'I am sorry, sir, our General Manager's name is Mr Tom Topman. You must have the wrong number.'

Call at a convenient time

Get to know the best time to call people. Try to anticipate the work habits of the person you are calling and avoid busy or inconvenient times such as coffee breaks or lunch meetings. Ask, 'Is it convenient to talk to you now or can I call you back later?'

For international calls, allow for differences in time zones and daylight saving times.

Be friendly, polite and helpful

Before calling, think of the person you are calling. Collect all the references you will need for the call. Make yourself comfortable, take a deep breath and 'put a smile into your voice'. Make an effort to sound friendly. A pleasant voice and a helpful attitude are often the first impressions the caller has of your organisation and could influence further business.

Listen for voice tones

Listen carefully for voice tones and inflections. With experience you should be able to tell if your contact sounds busy or preoccupied. If so, say, 'Are you busy? When can I call you back?'

Don't do all the talking

Pause from time to time. Give the other person a chance to think and respond.

Requests for information

If an inward call requires reference work or research, don't keep the caller waiting. Offer to locate the information and phone back at a specified time. Keep frequently used references handy to the telephone.

Handling complaints

If clients call with complaints, be sympathetic. Thank them for bringing the problem to your notice, offer to investigate and then call them back. Do not cover up with excuses. Investigate as soon as possible and phone back (with an apology, if necessary) thanking them for the call and state what you are going to do about the problem.

When calling long distance

Always tell the person who answers the telephone you are calling long distance. This encourages prompt attention. If your contact is not in, find out the best time to call back or leave a message to have the call returned, preferably at a stated time.

Wrong numbers

If you get the wrong number, apologise. If someone calls you by mistake, be pleasant about it.

Helpful phrases for switchboard operators

- *Answering an outside call*
  'Good morning. Triple Z Computers – Shirley Black speaking. Can I help you?'

- *Before extending a call*
  'One moment, please.'

- *If an extension is engaged*
  'I am sorry; the line is engaged. Do you wish to wait?'

- *If the caller is still waiting*
  'Thank you for waiting, Mr Ross. I am sorry. Mr Jones's line is still engaged. Do you wish to wait or can I take a message?'

- *When you terminate a call*
  'Thank you for calling, Mr Ross.'

- *If the extension does not answer*
  'I shall try again for you.' If still no reply, 'Could someone else help you or could I take a message?'

- *When you need to say who is calling*
  'May I say who is calling, please?'

- *To interrupt a local call for a long distance call*
  'Excuse me, Mr Jones, I have a long distance call for you. Will you take it?'

- *When answering an internal call*
  'Operator.' *Never* 'Hello' or 'Are you there?'

◀ PART 3 ▶

WRITE RIGHT

When you have read this part of the book you will be able to plan and write better messages. You will learn how to write concise reports, business letters, letters to editors of newspapers and newspaper articles. You will know how to prepare a curriculum vitae and how to apply for a job.

◄ 25. ►

ALL MESSAGES SHOULD BE PLANNED

Perhaps you have a secret desire to write a book, or maybe you have to write an article for a magazine or a report for your boss. Perhaps you want to make a public speech or give a talk on radio. Whatever your aim, the first thing you should do is to spend a few minutes planning exactly what you want to say and how you can say it most effectively. A little time spent planning can save you a great deal of time later. So before you start writing, start thinking.

Be clear about what you want to say.

If you are trying to promote an idea by means of a talk, an article or a report, ask yourself the following questions:

- What are the problems?
- What are the needs?
- What are the priorities?

The answers should help you to clarify the *purpose* of your message. With the purpose clearly in your mind, you can then continue to ask more questions:

- What do I want to say?
- To whom do I want to say it?
- How much do they already know about the subject?
- Will my message be relevant?

The answers will help you to assess the *background*. But before you start planning your strategy there are a few more questions to be answered:

- What information do I need?
- What do I need to do?

Preparing an action plan

It is a good idea at this stage to prepare an action plan setting out tasks, time required to complete them, target dates for their completion and any other information you need. (For example you may decide to list resource persons you wish to interview.) Figure 25.1 is an example.

Action plan			
Task	How this will be done	Time required	Target date

Figure 25.1 *How to set out an action plan*

Guidelines for writing your message

1. Decide on your purpose, aim or objective.
2. Summarise what you want to say.
3. Decide how you can best deal with the subject.
4. Prepare your action plan.
5. Collect all necessary information by research, interviews etc.
6. Write a draft, making sure you include all the important things you want to say.
7. Write an introduction and conclusion.
8. Add a good title.
9. Edit the script.
10. Ask a few colleagues to read the script and give constructive criticisms.
11. Test your message on some of the people who will be the end-users.
12. Review and rewrite where necessary.
13. Do a final edit.
14. Make sure the layout is simple and attractive.
15. Arrange for publication.

Whether your message is verbal or written, always try to evaluate it. You can always ask for feedback (or maybe just listen to comments), or you can carry out a formal evaluation. Both will tell you how you can improve your next effort so that you can modify your message or actions accordingly.

◀ 26. ▶

WRITE TO BE READ

Writing is easy as ABC:

    A. Know your readers
    B. Have a clear purpose
    C. Make a plan and follow it.

When people read they shouldn't have to make a big effort to understand. Good prose should carry the reader along as if in a boat gliding down a river; difficult prose has has the reader rowing against the current. Most people are lazy readers so if you want your writing to be read follow the simple rules outlined below.

Think about your readers before you start writing

Visualise your readers and write *for* them.

Decide who you are writing for. What do they want to read? Readers like to identify with the things they read. If you can identify with someone who will be reading your work, all the better. Pretend you are talking to them as you write.

Write to arouse your readers' interest. Stir their imagination. Start them thinking about their needs. Use a style that makes the reader think, 'This article was written for me'.

'If the writer does not understand the reader, the reader will never understand the writer.'

Outline and plan

Arrange statements in descending order of importance.

Prepare an outline of what you want to say. Arrange statements so that the most important one is first and the others flow on in logical order. You are then ready to write around the outline – to put 'flesh on the bones'.

Write crisply

Do not pad out the text.

Make your writing crisp, clear and concise. It isn't what you say, it's the way you say it that arouses your readers' interest.

Use simple words

Choose words familiar to your readers and write simply and concisely. Short words, phrases and sentences can be very effective. Consider this sentence:

'Jesus wept.'

114

When you have a choice of words use the simplest one:

Instead of . . .	*write . . .*
excavate	dig
contribute	give
purchase	buy
terminate	end
conceal	hide
attempt	try
possess	own
utilise	use

Use active words

Write with enthusiasm and vigour to make your writing lively. Use active words that are precise, strong and positive and will stir people to action.

Put action into your writing by using active verbs. (An active verb tells what the subject does; a passive verb tells what happens to the subject.) For example, 'The chairman called for a motion to adjourn' is stronger than 'A motion to adjourn was called for by the chairman'.

Be enthusiastic

To get enthusiasm from your readers, write with enthusiasm! Write about things which interest you and about which you feel strongly. Your writing should be full of energy. Use short, snappy sentences. Avoid long, laboured paragraphs. 'We don't need these goods – let's get rid of them', should get more action than 'These goods are surplus to our requirements and should be disposed of in due course'.

Talk directly to your reader

The more sentences you address to your reader, the greater the interest you will arouse:

'Why are you reading this article? Have you learnt anything so far?'

Develop your own style

There is no law to say you must write like everyone else. English is a flexible language. Don't worry, so long as your meaning is clear. Write to express, not to impress.

Use 'people' words

The more words about people, the more interesting your writing will be. Anecdotes, stories and emotions raise the interest level of readers.

Use dialogue

So you think dialogue is only for fiction writers? Not so. It can be used to express opinions and clarify statements and opinions. But how can you use it when nobody is talking? Let's see what we can do by rewriting that previous paragraph:

> 'You might say, "Dialogue is only for fiction writers." I could answer, "On the contrary, you can use it to express opinions and make your meanings clear if you are writing non-fiction".'

There's nothing wrong with imaginary conversations if they serve your purpose. So invent people, invent conversations.

Readers pay more attention when they see quotation marks. Use dialogue when you want to emphasise a special point. It will add variety to your writing and help your readers to remember.

Your opening paragraph

Don't cram all your facts into your opening paragraph. You should whet your readers' appetites with a tasty morsel or two so that they are eagerly awaiting the main course.

Draft first, 'polish' later

Write a rough draft. Get your ideas down. Leave the 'polishing' for later. Be prepared to write and rewrite several times until you are satisfied. Everything should be in logical order and the text should flow smoothly.

James Michener has admitted he rewrites chapters of his books as many as five or six times. He says, 'Talent is common but disciplined talent and perseverance not so common.' So, unless you have a good editor, be prepared for some hard work.

It's a good idea to ask a few appropriate people to read your text before you finally 'go to print'. Their constructive criticisms may help you to do a much better job.

Paragraphs

Have you noticed how effective a short sentence is when it follows a long one? This applies to paragraphs too. We need contrasts to break the monotony in writing. So vary the lengths of your paragraphs – but generally keep them short.

Edit, edit, edit

When your ideas are down on paper, chop and change and rearrange. Be ruthless – remove all unnecessary words and phrases. (To start with, see how many 'that's' you can remove.) 'Kill' those stock phrases our politicians love:

> . . . in order that (so)
> . . . in the near future (soon)
> . . . at this point in time (now)
> . . . in the event that (if)
> . . . for the purpose of (for)
> . . . for the reason that (because)
> . . . with the result that (so)
> . . . factual information (facts)
> . . . general public (public)
> . . . true facts (facts).

Punctuate for clarity. Make sure meanings are clear and there are no ambiguous statements. Finally, check spelling, grammar and punctuation.

Lively pages

There is nothing more daunting for a reader than long chapters with long paragraphs – page after page of solid blocks of black type. The printed page can be made visually interesting – lively in fact. Illustrations – photographs, drawings, cartoons – are a big help, but there are other ways:

- Use those punctuation marks on your typewriter
- Vary type styles and spacing
- Use underlining or capitals for emphasis
- Use subheadings
- Vary the length of paragraphs
- Use direct speech (and quotation marks)
- For casual asides use brackets
- Leave plenty of white space on your pages
- List points you want to make with large black dots or squares (as here).

Make your message memorable
Relevant anecdotes, stories and quotations raise the interest level and help readers to remember your message. Just because you have written a mass of facts you have not necessarily done a good job. You should present the facts so readers will want to read them and will remember them.

To summarise, the essentials for easy-to-read writing are to:

- arrange your thoughts in logical order
- be conversational
- use short simple, familiar words
- use personal words
- use active words
- be brief
- be positive
- use short, varied sentences
- use short paragraphs
- write with enthusiasm and feeling
- be sincere.

Non-sexist language

Keep your language neutral.

Writers often face a dilemma when trying to overcome problems of gender and to avoid sexist language. The English language lacks a 'unisex' third person singular pronoun, so some writers use 'he/she' (or even 's/he') and 'his/hers'. These are clumsy and interrupt the smooth flow of words in a sentence, especially if it has to be read aloud. Avoid them if possible but if you can't, try some of the following.

Use a gender-neutral term

Instead of . . .	write . . .
manpower	personnel
mankind	people
foreman	supervisor
postman	postal worker
to man	to operate, and so on.

Rewrite your statement in the plural

Instead of, 'Each pupil must bring his birth certificate', write, 'Pupils must bring their birth certificates'.

Instead of, 'Every trainer should prepare his or her own visual aids', write, 'All trainers should prepare their own visual aids'.

Address your reader directly in the second person

Instead of, 'The candidate must bring his own calculator', write, 'Bring your own calculator'.

Replace third person singular possessives with articles

Instead of, 'Each committee member expressed his opinion', write, 'Each committee member expressed an opinion'.

Repeat titles

Instead of, 'The Minister of Health will, at his discretion, make recommendations to the Prime Minister', write, 'The Minister of Health will, at the Minister's discretion, make recommendations to the Prime Minister'.

If nothing else sounds right put the sentence in the passive voice

Instead of, 'Each officer presented his report', write, 'Reports were presented by each officer'.

Remember

It *is* possible to avoid sexist writing but it may take a little thought and effort to rearrange your sentences.

◀ 27. ▶

WRITING REPORTS

To write a report, it is first necessary to collect information, analyse it, and then write up the results.

Sooner or later you will find you are asked to write a report. It may be a business report, the report of a meeting or the analysis of a situation. It need not be the ordeal many fear; it can be an interesting and exhilarating experience. It's a chance for you to offer vigorous and thought-provoking ideas. Like many other things, it is not difficult if you break it down into small tasks.

Your first task is to collect all the available information. Thomas Edison advised, 'Find out everything everybody else knows, and then begin where they left off.' Don't rely on libraries and data printouts alone. Look at the files in your own office. Remember, 'The wheel is being reinvented every day.'

With this background information, you can decide what you want to accomplish in your report. Start by thinking about who is going to read it. Then aim at defining the problems, making statements and supporting them with evidence, and, finally, giving solutions or making recommendations.

The master plan

Action to be taken.

- Clearly identify what you are required to do. Make sure your terms of reference are clear.

- Who's going to read the report? How busy are they? When is it required?

- As ideas occur to you, write them down.

- A simple way to record information (and to keep it brief) is to use cards or half sheets of paper. Head each piece with a main topic title and add facts as you come across them in your reading. The topics are then easy to arrange in logical order.

- Prepare your plan of attack. If it is necessary to interview people, make a list of questions.

- If your time is limited, plan carefully. Allow plenty of time for producing your report – remember, it always takes longer than you think.

Preparing your report

Collect all related material from files, libraries, interviews and retrieval systems. Be ruthless. Sift the relevant from the irrelevant quickly but keep a record of references for all source material. Often you need to go back for additional information.

Collect information.

Organising your material

When you have collected all the material you require, arrange it in a logical order. Don't confuse facts and opinions. If it is a fact say so; if it is an opinion, assess its value. Good information goes into the body of the report; supporting material is put in the annex or appendix.

Organise what you have collected.

Writing your report

Officials place great faith in reports. Their time is valuable, so keep your report brief, to the point, and easy to read. Follow this basic structure for a well set out and comprehensive report:

Draft first.

1. Title
2. Table of contents
3. Abstract (or summary)
4. Introduction
5. Main body
6. Conclusions
7. Recommendations

8. Acknowledgements
9. References
10. Appendices (or annexes)

1. Title
- Make the title factual, clear and brief.
- Consider the needs of computer-based information systems by including key words.
- Preferably use fewer than 12 words (or 100 letters).
- The title page should include details of the author and the name and address of the organisation publishing the report.
- Don't forget the date!
- For small 'internal' reports add a circulation list.

2. Table of contents
List all the major headings and subheadings, appendices and illustrations, with page numbers.

3. Abstract (or summary)
Write this last. It is really a mini-report giving the basic facts of the problem, the evidence and the conclusions. It should be a single paragraph of approximately 200 words.

Sometimes it is put on the front page of the report.

4. Introduction
State the purpose of the report. The introduction usually includes the terms of reference and defines the reason the report was written.

5. Main body
The material should be arranged logically according to the purpose of the report. It should be easy to read. It should give a comprehensive and systematic review of the problem, the evidence, the issues and the possibilities. There should be a logical sequence of facts and ideas leading the reader from topic to topic.

Careful paragraphing, subheadings and numbering will help readers to remember the various points raised and the way the argument has been developed.

Attractive layout creates a good first impression and encourages reading. A suggested layout is as follows:

1.0 MAJOR HEADING

1.1 SUBHEADING
  1.11 MINOR HEADING
  1.12 MINOR HEADING

2.0 MAJOR HEADING etc

6. Conclusions

Busy people may read only the conclusions and the recommendations; therefore they should be simple, concise and complete.

The conclusions should be clear statements derived logically from the main body of the report and supported by relevant evidence.

They should be arranged in order of importance and should relate to the purpose of the report.

7. Recommendations

Recommendations for future action should be stated simply, clearly and concisely. Make sure they are positive and practical. They should be numbered in order of importance or logic.

Sometimes, if they are considered very important and of wide interest, the recommendations are 'extracted' and put at the beginning of the report.

8. Acknowledgements

These are sometimes put before the table of contents. Look at other reports to see which position is preferred by the people who have requested your report.

Thank people or institutions for their help in the preparation of your report. Be sincere.

9. References
For books, list:

> Author (or authors): name first and initials, full title for corporate authors
> Title of book
> Name of publisher
> Date of publication and edition
> Number of pages
> International Standard Book Number (ISBN)
> Page references if required.

For journals, list:

> Author or authors (name first and initials, full title for corporate authors)
> Title of article
> Title of periodical
> Volume and part number
> Date and year of publication
> Page references.

10. Appendices (annexes)
This section should contain supporting material such as sets of data, details of methods used, graphs and illustrations. The material should be chosen and presented with the same care and logic as the rest of the report. Appendices are not a dumping ground to fill out the report.

Revising your report

Revise your draft, incorporating any comments you agree with.

You haven't finished yet! Now you have a script, it needs 'polishing'.

First, photocopy two or three extra copies well spaced with wide margins. If possible, ask a colleague who is familiar with the subject, someone from a related discipline and maybe someone who could give a general reader's point of view, to write their comments on the script. Consider their comments carefully and incorporate those that you agree with.

Next, put the report aside for a few days. Meanwhile you could prepare a mailing list and covering letters.

Checking the report

When you return to your report, read it straight through as if you have never seen it before. Then answer these questions:

- Does the title tell you what it's about?
- Does the table of contents include everything required for quick reference?
- Does the introduction state accurately and concisely why the report was written and what it contains?
- Does the body of the report give the facts in logical order?
- Are all the statements factual and clearly expressed?
- Are headings brief and descriptive?
- Are photographs, diagrams, charts etc inserted in the most appropriate places?
- Is the abstract or summary brief, clear and honest?
- Are the arguments objective and accurate?
- Do the conclusions interpret the data in the report honestly?
- Are the recomendations positive and practical?
- Are the appendices relevant?
- Are the references useful for anyone wanting further information?
- Is the layout consistent?

If you are satisfied that it is a good report, the script is ready for final typing.

Check the report once more.

Attractive presentation

An attractive cover makes a good first impression. If possible, get an interesting cover page printed or purchase special folders for the report.

Ensure the report has an attractive appearance.

Follow-up

If you have written a report recommending changes, don't take it for granted that the key people will have read your report. Make an appointment with them to discuss your report and let them ask questions about your recommendations. Such follow-up appointments often make all the difference between reports which have their recommendations implemented and those which are just filed away and forgotten.

Discuss your report with the key readers to ensure its recommendations or findings are not ignored.

125

◄ 28. ►

BETTER BUSINESS LETTERS

Business letters should be brief, simple and direct.

Business letters should be well planned. References to previous correspondence should be quoted. The letter should have an opening for the reader, a middle that gives the message and an ending that offers the writer's help or expresses hope for future business.

The opening paragraph

Make the subject apparent at the start, using a heading if appropriate.

The opening paragraph should be short and used to identify the subject matter:

'Thank you for your request for information about our new personal computer.'

The message

The message should be clear.

The message should get to the point quickly in plain language using short sentences and short paragraphs:

'We are happy to send you a booklet containing the information you will need to evaluate our new computer. The section on page 10 sets out questions and answers for users. When you have read this section you will see its advantages over other models.'

Ensure the reader knows what result you expect.

The closure

Finish with a direct statement, using active verbs if possible. Offer

126

further help or express a hope for further business:

'If we can help you in any way, please do not hesitate to contact me.'

The rules of good business writing

- Set out references, addresses, names and dates clearly.
- Keep your messages brief.
- Get to the point quickly.
- Use plain language. Don't use jargon or clichés.
- Keep your sentences and paragraphs short.
- Be firm, positive and helpful.

Parts of a business letter

1. The return address
2. The date
3. Receiver's address
4. Greeting or salutation
5. Subject reference
6. The opening paragraph
7. The message
8. The closure
9. Courteous ending
10. The signature block, containing (i) the signature (ii) the writer's name and (iii) official position.

Checklist.

Check these points in your letters. They are illustrated in Figure 28.1 (overleaf).

Letters to sell a product

Do your homework before you write a sales letter.

Sales letters.

First learn as much as you can about your product!

- What can it do?
- What are its main features?
- How does it differ from its competitors?
- How much will it sell for?
- What materials is it made from?

127

1.

TRIPLE ZZZ COMPUTERS
SUITE 301, JAYMAC BUILDING, AVON QUAY, BRISTOL BS1 1KP

2.

10 May 1993

3.

Mr RU Shaw
Manager
XYZ Associates Limited
PO Box 123
Bristol BS99 9JL

4.

Dear Mr Shaw

5.

REQUEST FOR COMPUTER INFORMATION
Your letter P/S.33 dated 8 May 1993

6.

Thank you for your request for information about our new personal computer.

7.

We are sending you a booklet containing the information you will need to evaluate our new computer. The section on page 10 sets out questions and answers for users. When you have read this section you will see its advantages over other models.

8.

If we can help you in any way do not hesitate to contact me.

9.

Yours sincerely

10.

Robin Jay
Manager

Figure 28.1 *Example of a business letter*

Next research the market. Analyse potential customers. Where do they live? What is their average income? Get the reaction to your product of a representative sample of the group.

After you have done your homework thoroughly you are ready to write your sales letter.

Sales letter strategy
Aim to develop a sequence of ideas.

1. *Catch the reader's attention*
   'Cut your electricity bills in half.'

2. *Stimulate the reader's interest*
   'Our new energy/solar water heaters have a revolutionary design. They will burn waste materials, such as paper and plastic bags and they use solar energy. They have no working parts to go wrong.'

3. *Develop a desire for your product*
   Aim for the response, 'I would like to have one of those.'
   'Just think what you could do with the extra money. It's like a pay rise.'

4. *Encourage action*
   'If you mail the enclosed card today our representative will telephone and make an appointment to call to discuss your needs. You are under no obligation.'

Letters to deal with complaints

Letters dealing with complaints should be polite and helpful and end on a friendly note.

Soothe the feelings of those who write to complain, and thank them. They have indicated a possible weakness in your organisation which you can rectify.

The opening paragraph
The opening paragraph should identify the problem or request and show that you agree in principle with the person's right to complain or request something:

'Thank you for bringing the problem to our notice. It is only by such actions we can improve our service to our clients.'

129

The message
If you have to refuse a request:

1. *Give reasons*

   If your refusal is based on good reasons, state these clearly. Take the reader into your confidence. Do not talk down to clients:

   'We have sold 1,000 of those motors during the last two years without a single complaint.'

2. *Give a clear refusal*

   The refusal should follow logically from the reasons given:

   'We are not prepared to refund your money because you have had six months' use of the machine and we suspect that the servicing has been at fault.'

The closure
End on a positive note showing a concern for your client:

'If you could bring the motor in to our workshop we will overhaul it and charge you only for replacement parts. We hope we can solve this problem to our mutual satisfaction.'

Letters to collect debts

Letters chasing overdue payments. Make an effort to maintain goodwill even if a debt is long overdue. The collection process goes through distinct stages. The first and second letters can be used as reminders. It's diplomatic to assume the customer has overlooked payment and will pay when reminded. The third letter can take the form of an enquiry. You can ask for an explanation of the circumstances that prevent payment. If there is no satisfactory explanation, a fourth letter should demand urgent action.

However, few companies let bills go unpaid this long, and a short, sharp shock is usually administered in the form of a summons to court giving particulars of the debt or a visit from a debt-collecting agency after two months.

The reminder
Assume the customer has overlooked the bill:

'This is a friendly reminder that your account is overdue. Perhaps you have posted your cheque already. If so, thank you.'

Strong reminder

Assume the customer has overlooked paying. Reassure the customer that credit is still available.

'Most of our customers appreciate a reminder when their account is overdue. You may have already posted payment. If so, thank you. If not, will you please do so at your earliest convenience. We look forward to being of service to you in the future.'

Enquiry or explanation stage

By this time you assume there is a reason why the customer has not paid. Try appealing to the customer's pride by suggesting they avoid the embarrassment of a bad credit record. Appeal to their self-interest by reminding them of the value of credit:

'Please contact us immediately if you find you are unable to pay. Together we should be able to work something out.'

If you receive a satisfactory explanation, there is a good chance payment will eventually be made.

This letter is often combined with the first, gentle reminder.

Urgency or final stage

Impress on the customer the seriousness of the situation. Try not to threaten, but point out what the customer has to lose if the bill is not paid. Be demanding and stress immediate action. At this point you might imply the possibility of legal action rather than state it.

'Please send your cheque *immediately*, or contact us so a payment plan can be arranged. Please respond within seven days.

◀ 29. ▶

WORKING WITH THE MEDIA

Do your utmost to get free publicity.

If you want to publicise your business or cause, you will have to take the initiative and contact someone in 'the media'. You have four main choices: newspapers, radio, television, periodicals (journals and magazines). Your choice will depend on the kind of people you want to reach, the type of message you want to get across, how much detail you want in it and how urgent it is.

Newspapers reach almost everyone in the community. They are produced quickly and can print detailed information which can be kept for recall.

Radio also reaches a large audience but it can get the message across more rapidly. Radio messages are short and, once they have been broadcast, they are not easily recalled.

Television reaches a vast audience with people of all ages, backgrounds and interests. The message is both visual and aural but, like radio, is not easily recalled (unless transferred to video).

Periodicals, magazines and journals are most suitable for in-depth messages. With them, your audience is more specific, so you will reach the people most likely to be interested in your topic. Articles for periodicals and journals should be well researched and have good illustrations – there is usually plenty of space for graphics. Unfortunately, there is usually a frustrating time lag between the writing of the article and its appearance in print.

Helping the reporter

The reporter's job is to gather and report news. Try to understand the difficulties of the job and the struggle to meet deadlines set by the editor.

Get to know the reporters so you can establish a good working relationship which will be of mutual benefit. Be honest with them and work to develop a mutual trust.

If you want help and publicity for your organisation, keep the media informed of its activities. Give them as much advance notice as possible of coming events. Be prepared to do your homework and supply copy if you have a message you want putting across. Make your message as clear and concise as possible, but also provide background material.

Make the reporter's job easier in the following ways:

- Always type your material
- Type on one side of the paper only
- Double space the typing and leave wide margins
- Leave a large space at the top of the first page
- Number the pages clearly
- Never break a paragraph going from one page to another
- Put your name and telephone number on the first page.

Be cooperative

If a reporter wants a story, try to help. Give information as quickly as possible, unless it is a controversial subject and you want time to consider. In that case, ask them to call back at a specified time – and have your answer ready.

Provide information or comment in good times and bad, when you are asked, and build a reputation for reliability.

Make sure all information you give to the media is accurate. If you don't know an answer, say so. Offer to find out and call them back or tell them where to go to get the information.

If you say you will call back at a certain time, keep your word. Remember, journalists have strict deadlines to meet.

If you want publicity, make it as easy as possible for reporters by giving them all the information they need. If you help them they will help you. If they are seeking information from you, supply them with short accurate reports. If you need time to research a topic, tell them when you will be ready to give an interview or supply copy. Make sure you do your homework and have it ready on time. Be friendly and courteous at all times.

Foster good relationships

Good relationships do not just happen. They have to be worked at.

You must be prepared to work hard at good relationships with the media. You can prepare your material well and give reporters good leads, good briefings and accurate background information. But do not assume too much. Often misreporting occurs because people do not take time to explain what they really mean.

If you are misquoted, don't rush to the editor or the manager of the radio or television station. Contact the reporter first and try to discuss the problem in a friendly manner. If you storm in to the editor, the journalist will feel betrayed and you will lose his or her respect and trust as well as friendship.

Coverage of events

Inform the media well in advance of any planned events.

If you want successful coverage of an event, notify the local media about it as soon as possible. Send them any advance information, such as the programme and information about speakers and their topics. Indicate how many people might be present and the types of people coming.

On the day of the event, make sure tables, chairs and reading lamps are set out for the journalists near the speaker's platform, so they can see and hear well. Supply them with detailed programmes, background information and anything else they require. If possible make a room available where they can type up their copy and collect copies of the speaker's papers. Arrange for someone to be available to help them and act as their hosts.

Aim for good media relations – it takes time and effort, but it will pay dividends.

Hints from experienced journalists

The reporters' views.

'Never say "No comment" unless you want a full investigation carried out.'

134

'Being unprepared is a sure way to a bad press. When you come out of a meeting, know how you will answer tricky questions.'

'You can kill criticism and rumours with a timely, honest, factual story. Hard facts stop speculation.'

'Don't be afraid if a reporter uses a tape recorder. It will help to get your story right.'

◄ 30. ►

WRITING FOR NEWSPAPERS

The basic principles of writing are the same whether you are writing a speech, a report or a newspaper article. You must know who your audience is and what they want to know. The facts must be collected conscientiously and organised logically. Then you must get your ideas across as clearly and concisely as you can, using good, simple English.

List items in descending order of importance.

When you write for a newspaper, remember – news is about people. Newspapers reach a large audience, so aim to interest and involve as many of them as possible. Make sure they are able to relate to what you write.

The inverted pyramid

When you have collected all the facts for your article, arrange them in order of importance. The basic format of a newspaper article is referred to by journalists as the inverted pyramid, illustrated in Figure 30.1.

There are two main reasons for this format. First, readers may start an article but for one reason or another never get past the first few paragraphs. Even if they stop reading at the end of the first paragraph, they will have read the most important facts. Second, if the story is too long, the editor can easily cut the last few paragraphs. The reader still receives the main message and the most important facts.

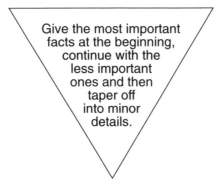

Figure 30.1 *The inverted pyramid*

The 'intro'

It is often a good idea to write the whole article and then go back and rewrite the introduction. This so-called 'intro' should grab the reader's attention and, with the inverted pyramid format, the key facts will be stated clearly at the beginning.

The introduction summarises the article and a reviewer may quote it verbatim.

The body

The body of the story should answer the questions:

Checklist.

Who?
What?
Why?
When?
Where?
How?
(And how much will it cost?)

Make sure you give all the facts.

When these have been written in logical order, read the article critically and be prepared to rewrite it.

Edit it. Cut it down – remove all unnecessary words. Correct grammar, punctuation and spelling. Make sure the story flows well.

137

Good English

Write well and succinctly, and address the reader directly.

Use short words, short sentences and short paragraphs. Try to keep one idea per sentence.

Use active sentences. English verbs have two voices, the active and the passive. In the active voice, the subject does something; in the passive voice the subject is being acted upon. Compare 'The editor read the story' (active) with 'The story was read by the editor' (passive). Use the active voice where possible – it makes your writing more lively and interesting.

Write in a personal manner. Authors in scientific journals often use the impersonal, for example, 'It was found that . . .' For newspapers, it is better to write. 'We found that . . .'

Be specific in your writing. Avoid vague words such as 'adequate' or 'enough'. Get rid of jargon and clichés.

Layout

Double space the lines and leave wide margins. Recheck the text before sending.

Good layout could make all the difference between an article which is accepted and one that is rejected. Editors and sub-editors are busy people and do not have time to struggle with untidy, cramped or confused copy.

Put your name and telephone number on the top of the first page. Leave the first half page blank for the sub-editor's notes and instructions.

Give a short working title to your article. Type on one side of the paper only. Use double spacing and leave wide margins. Number your pages clearly, and do not break paragraphs between pages.

Meet deadlines with clean copy.

Illustrations

Illustrations have wide appeal. They need captions, so provide them.

Photographs and diagrams attract attention and add interest.

Photographs should be clear with strong contrast. Show only essentials, so try to take photographs with a plain background. Make sure the subject almost fills the photograph. Check whether the editor prefers a negative or a black and white print.

Write a full caption on a label and stick it to the back of the illustration.

Read *How to Write Articles for Profit and PR* by Mel Lewis (Kogan Page).

◄ 31. ►

LETTERS TO THE EDITOR

You can often get free publicity for your ideas by writing letters to the editors of prestigious and influential newspapers. Here are some guidelines:

- State you ideas or complaint clearly at the beginning of your letter.

- Don't be offensive. You will make more impact with restrained language than with abuse.

- Use humour and satire. They often hit where it hurts most.

- Avoid topics such as religion and racial controversy, blasphemy and issues which could be libellous.

- Arrange your statements in logical order. Start with an attention-grabbing introduction and your strongest argument. Leave your weaker arguments till later because that is the part that will be left out if the letter is too long.

- Keep your sentences and paragraphs short.

- When you have drafted your letter, 'boil it down'. Remove all jargon and clichés and all unnecessary words.

◄ 32. ►

WRITING FOR MAGAZINES

Homework first

As with all serious writing, it pays to do your homework first to get background information.

Research the market.

If you have an idea for a story, select a magazine that prints similar types of stories. Make a précis of your proposed article and see if the editor is interested. This can save you much work. You don't know what other articles they have filed waiting to be published. If the editor is interested you will be given guidelines and told how many words are required and when the article is needed.

Useful guidelines

Many magazines have printed guidelines for authors. They will send you copies on request and these can be very helpful. *The Economist* guidelines include the following:

Write in a style the particular journal finds acceptable.

'On only two scores can *The Economist* hope to outdo its rivals consistently. One is the quality of its analysis; the other is the quality of its writing ... Keep in mind George Orwell's six elementary rules.

1. Never use a metaphor, simile or other figure of speech which you are used to seeing in print.
2. Never use a long word where a short one will do.
3. If it is possible to cut out a word, always cut it out.
4. Never use the passive where you can use the active.

141

5. Never use a foreign phrase, a scientific word or a jargon word if you can think of an everyday English equivalent.

6. Break any of these rules sooner than say anything outright barbarous.'

The *Reader's Digest* in their notes to authors state:

'A *Digest* story should reward readers in some way – either emotionally, by sharing a powerful story, or with useful, practical information, or by bringing an urgent national issue into clear focus and offering solutions.'

People are interested in other people's emotions and ideas, so be prepared to share yours with others.

Plan your article

Draft the article, then check and sense it before sending.

- Write an outline of your article.
- Try a dramatic lead-in to your story. Anecdotes, if brief, can be very effective.
- State your theme clearly early in your article.
- Make sure your facts and figures are correct – double check, as your credibility is at stake.
- Use active, lively words to make your story interesting.
- Use simple words to paint vivid word pictures.
- Cut out clichés, unsupported claims, excessive enthusiasm and exaggerated emotions.
- Revise, rewrite and edit until your article sounds right when you read it aloud. Coleridge described good prose as 'words in their best order'. Chop and change and rearrange until your writing sounds right to your ear.
- Check that your article is the required length.

Keep trying

Learn from rejections and improve your approach.

Don't let rejection slips discourage you – look upon them as learning slips. If you have something to say plan it, write it, edit it, polish it and redraft it again and again until you get it right. Keep trying and keep learning from your successes and rejections.

◀ 33. ▶

APPLYING FOR A JOB

The first thing you should do when applying for a job is to prepare your personal fact sheet (also called your curriculum vitae or CV).

Personal fact sheet

This should include your:

The CV enables you to present yourself in the best possible light.

- Full name and address
- Telephone number – day and night
- Nationality
- Age, date and place of birth
- Marital status
- Educational qualifications
- Work experience:

    Dates, names and addresses of employers, type of work, your responsibilities and accomplishments
    Holiday work
    Voluntary work
    Give details of skills relevant to the job you are applying for, eg computer, word processing or foreign language skills.

- Hobbies, sports and interests
- Leadership experiences, in sport, youth groups, community projects, etc

- Give names, addresses and phone numbers of three people who can supply references. (Be sure to contact these people first to get their permission.)

Presentation is important

A CV must be well presented.

Make sure your fact sheet is typed neatly and is well set out with headings and columns for dates etc. Employ an experienced typist if necessary. It should be typed on good-quality white or off-white bond paper.

Keep it simple and as short as possible.

Attach a recent photograph of yourself. A passport size is ideal – one where you are smartly dressed.

Attach photocopies of appropriate certificates and references. Do not send originals but take them to an interview.

Covering letter

Send the CV with a covering letter addressed to a named person.

If you are applying for an advertised job or sending a personal fact sheet to a prospective employer, your covering letter should, preferably, be neatly hand-written.

If possible, find out the name of the manager or personnel manager of the company from the switchboard operator. Figure 33.1 is an example of a letter.

The interview

You have only one chance to make a good first impression, so don't throw it away.

If you are successful with your letter and fact sheet and get a job interview, here are some guidelines:

- Do your homework. Find out about the organisation you are hoping to join. Annual reports are a good starting point. Talk to staff. Make an appointment and find out what they do – employment officers can be helpful.

- Dress suitably – the way they would want you to be dressed if you were working for them. Don't wear dark glasses.

- Be punctual. Arrive early so you can relax and be composed for the interview. Often a walk before the interview helps you relax.

Your address
and telephone number

Name of employer   Date
Title
Department
Company
Address

Dear Mr . . . or Ms . . .

I wish to apply for the position of . . . as advertised in . . .

I am enclosing the completed application form, my personal fact sheet, etc . . .

(*Then a paragraph about your present situation.*)

I am currently employed at . . .

or

I am finishing school or university on . . .

(*Then a paragraph about why you are looking for a job and why you are suitable for this particular job.*)

(*Then a paragraph about your relevant qualifications, abilities and interests – but keep it brief.*)

I would appreciate the opportunity to discuss the position further at an interview.

I look forward to hearing from you.

Yours sincerely (*if employer has been named*)

or

Yours faithfully

Signature

Figure 33.1 *Example of a job application covering letter*

- Take references, fact sheet and certificates in case they are needed, but don't flaunt them.

- Be polite. Wait until you are asked to sit. Sit up straight – no smoking or chewing gum. Smile, be friendly and natural – don't put on an act.

- If your interviewers ask, tell them why you would like to work with them and what you hope to contribute. If you do not understand a question say so. Be modest and honest. If you cannot do a job say you are willing to learn.

- Show you are enthusiastic and keen to get the job.

- Don't take over the interview. Let the interviewer ask the questions. Think before you answer a question. Try to answer concisely and be prepared to amplify if asked. Don't talk too much.

- Your job is to sell yourself. Be friendly, be natural, be enthusiastic about both your work and outside interests. Show you are an interesting person.

PART 4

MEET WITH SUCCESS

After you have read this part of the book you will be able to chair an effective meeting and bring about changes in an organisation. You will know the duties of a secretary and how to organise a large conference or convention.

'Every meeting has four main bones.
There are the wish bones –
the ones who wish someone
else will do all the work.

There are the jaw bones,
who do all the talking.

There are the knuckle bones.
They knock everything constructive
that others suggest.

Then there are the back bones –
they do all the work.'

◀ 34. ▶

FORMS OF ADDRESS

There has been much controversy in recent years over the correct method of addressing (and referring to) the person who coordinates or moderates at a meeting. Traditionally this person was the 'chairman' but now 'chairperson' is accepted. 'Chair' is also used widely, especially for the office itself.

Addressing the chair

During a meeting, all comments, questions and motions should be addressed to the chair. The preferred forms of address are 'Mister Chairman' or 'Madam Chair'.

Office bearers

Office bearers should be addressed by their title.

> 'Madam Secretary, please read the minutes.'
> 'Would the Treasurer please present the financial statement.'

Reference to other people is usually made in the third person:

> 'Madam Chair, the last speaker made a mistake. He said . . .'

Addressing a mixed audience

When addressing a mixed audience use 'Ladies and Gentlemen'. Remember, in this case the singular of 'Ladies' is 'Madam' (not 'Lady') and the singular of 'Gentlemen' is 'Sir'.

THE ROLE AND DUTIES OF A CHAIRPERSON

What a chairperson does.

Milton Berle once described a committee as 'a group of people who keep minutes and waste hours'. Make sure that your committees and meetings do not waste those precious hours.

Time spent preparing for a meeting is a sound investment. Do your homework; become familiar with the constitution or bylaws. Make sure you know the minimum number (quorum) that must be present before you can start business at a meeting. Know the correct voting procedures and whether notices of motions need to be given prior to the meeting (and if so how many days before).

The chair should remain neutral during debates, act as a referee and keep order according to the rules. Impartiality will earn respect and ensure that things get done in a fair and democratic fashion.

The chair should not dominate the meeting. A good chair should remain calm if tempers are frayed and keep a sense of humour. The chair should get the feeling of the meeting, summarise often to keep the meeting on track, and try to get the meeting to agree on important issues and to reach conclusions so things can swing into action.

You should:

Checklist.

- Prepare the meeting agenda with the secretary
- Make sure the secretary has given due notice of the meeting to all members

- Read the minutes of the previous meeting to see what business needs following up
- Start (and finish) on time
- See whether a quorum is present
- Call the meeting to order
- Keep to the agenda
- Keep speakers within the rules of the meeting procedures
- Preserve order and courtesy
- Prevent irrelevant and repetitious discussions
- Call upon speakers in the correct sequence after they have indicated they wish to speak
- Remain neutral
- After the meeting follow up and coordinate to see that things get done.

You should not:

- Infringe members' rights as defined in the constitution and bylaws
- Lose your temper
- Show bias
- Refuse motions. But you may rule for or against the following motions:
    'That the question not now be put'
    'That the matter be referred to a committee'
    'That the debate be adjourned'
    'That the meeting now adjourn'
    'That the chair's ruling be dissented from'
    'That the meeting no longer has confidence in the chair'.

Actions a chairperson should avoid.

You may:

- Appoint committees
- Decide on points of order
- Exercise a casting vote, if you want to.

◄ 36. ►

TEN GOLDEN RULES FOR BETTER MEETINGS

Ten rules.

1. Call a meeting only when it is necessary.
2. Plan your meeting well.
3. Prepare and distribute an agenda.
4. Remember time is valuable.
5. Keep control.
6. Get things done.
7. Make the most of the talent and experience present.
8. Review and summarise often.
9. Record recommendations and give members responsibilities for specific tasks.
10. Evaluate objectively.

Rule 1. Call a meeting only when it is necessary

Do not hold unnecessary meetings; they waste time.

Why are you going to hold a meeting? Meetings are held for different reasons. Here are some examples.

Meetings to share information

Meetings to announce new ventures, share news and keep people informed about what is going on, make people feel part of a team. They can also stop the spread of rumours which could harm the organisation.

Meetings to review progress

Meetings that report on progress are good for the morale of staff

152

working on a lengthy project or people working in different areas towards a common goal.

Team briefing meetings

Many organisations hold regular meetings to pass information down from top management and up from the workforce to top management. Staff are divided into groups with a leader who reports news items, production successes, deadlines, personnel changes and policy changes to top management. In turn, top management reports items from board meetings relevant to staff, to these leaders who take them back to their groups. Team briefing meetings are additional to an organisation's normal communication channels.

Meetings to generate ideas

Have a brainstorming meeting if you want to create something new, change direction or promote unconventional ideas and you want to involve as many people as possible.

Hints for conducting a brainstorming meeting
1. First, explain that brainstorming helps people to think creatively before starting to sort out priorities and decide whether things are possible. There should be no criticism of ideas. No one should worry about whether the ideas are practicable or not – they just put forward any ideas that come into their heads.

2. Tell the meeting precisely what subject you want them to discuss. Write it down for all to see.

3. Choose an enthusiastic person to lead and get someone to record all ideas on a board, overhead projector or large paper pad. (The writing must be visible to all present.)

4. Call for ideas. Don't allow interruptions or criticisms – just let the ideas flow freely and don't worry if some ideas seem crazy.

5. Examine each idea for immediate or future use.

6. Choose the best suggestion.

7. Discuss implications.

8. Plan the action.

Meetings to solve problems

When things go wrong a meeting can often be called to look for a solution. Do not look for scapegoats. Look for alternative ways of doing things and choose the most acceptable one. Again, brainstorming can be used very successfully.

Hints for conducting a problem-solving meeting
1. Make sure the problem is clearly defined and understood.
2. Make a list of its causes.
3. Try to get as many solutions as possible.
4. Examine each idea and then choose the best one.
5. Plan the action.
6. Discuss how various concerned groups will react to the plan.
7. If necessary, revise and summarise the plan.
8. Make recommendations.

Executive meetings

An executive (or a board) is usually elected to meet regularly to conduct business and to manage the affairs of an organisation between annual general meetings.

Read *How to Make Meetings Work* by Malcolm Peel (Kogan Page).

Rule 2. Plan your meeting well

As a practical exercise, copy Table 36.1 and fill in your answers before your next meeting.

Meetings must be well planned.

Table 36.1 *Planning a meeting*

Why am I calling this meeting?	
What do I hope to achieve?	
What sort of meeting would be best?	
Who can contribute?	
Approximately how many will attend?	
When is the best time?	
Where is the best place?	
How much time can we afford?	
How are we going to let people know about the meeting?	

When you have answered all the questions and informed all the people involved, you are then ready to write the agenda.

An agenda helps to ensure that members come prepared with the right information.

Rule 3. Prepare and distribute an agenda

You can reduce the duration of a meeting by having preliminary discussions with leading members of the group. They can help in the preparation of the agenda and in clarifying objectives.

An agenda is simply a list of business items to be considered at a meeting. The sequence of items on an agenda is important. Get your meeting 'warmed up' before you start on the more serious issues. An agenda could include:

- Time and place of the meeting
- Objectives of the meeting
- Time the meeting is due to finish
- Meal arrangements
- Names of participants and their positions
- List of topics or problems to be discussed, or presentations to be made
- Background papers and reports
- Expected outcomes of the meeting.

Here is a typical formal agenda:

1. Chairperson's opening remarks
2. Attendance and apologies
3. Approval of minutes of the last meeting
4. Matters arising from the minutes
5. Inward and outward correspondence
6. Financial statement and accounts for payment
7. Working party or subcommittee reports
8. Other reports
9. Motions (of which due notice has been given)
10. General business (at the discretion of the chair)
11. Date and arrangements for the next meeting

Experienced chairpersons usually have their own personal agendas setting out times for each activity and including memory-jogging notes.

Rule 4. Remember time is valuable

If you start a meeting late you will probably finish late. Give a warning, then start on time. Meetings are costly. (You can calculate the cost on the basis of numbers present, average salaries and the meeting time plus travelling time.) Control interruptions and deviations; strong leadership can stop people wandering off the subject.

When you open up a major issue try imposing a two-minute silence to give people time to think. Another alternative is to announce the topic and let people talk in pairs for a few minutes to clarify their ideas before you start formal discussions. These techniques can save time in the long run.

Finish on time. Adjourn the meeting as scheduled so others do not have their plans upset. Placing important items early on the agenda ensures that if any are not finished they will be the least important ones.

There is a tendency to waste time on unimportant issues if people at a meeting are getting tired. If this happens, adjourn the meeting or call a coffee break.

Allow more time than necessary for tea/coffee breaks. These can be shortened if you need to make up time.

Keep to the agenda. 'We are here to . . . The purpose of this meeting is . . . The next point to be decided is . . . '

Rule 5. Keep control

To keep control a chairperson must know the rules, give clear directions, listen carefully, summarise often and keep on schedule. Here are some hints if you have to chair a meeting:

- Know your authority. Be familiar with the constitution, bylaws or standing orders of the organisation.
- Do not sit in the 'chair' until you are about to begin the meeting.
- Start on time. Call the meeting to order – use a gavel if you have one or rap your pen on the table.
- Make a formal announcement. 'I declare this (weekly) meeting of the . . . open.' This is significant because the business of the meeting is recorded from this point onwards. A formal announcement sets the tone of a meeting.

- Welcome all members and make introductions. This act is often overlooked but it is a matter of courtesy and makes people feel that they are expected to contribute to the meeting.

- Make sure all have a copy of the agenda.

- The larger the meeting the more formal you will need to be. Most small business meetings are very informal.

- Take notes, even if they are only key words, so you can summarise frequently.

- Questions and comments should be directed to the chair or through the chair rather than back and forth across the table. This is important if you are to retain control.

- You have a responsibility to ration the time available and to keep the meeting focused on the agenda and objectives.

- Be sensitive to individuals. Encourage all members to contribute. Shy or quiet people must be invited to participate: 'What do you think of the idea, Helen?' Restrain people who tend to overparticipate: 'Bill, let's hear what Mary has to say before we go on.' A skilful leader has a talent for involving quiet individuals while restraining those who tend to monopolise the discussions.

- Make sure tasks are clear. If you are discussing a problem, state the problem clearly. Tell the meeting what is required – a decision, a new plan, some suggestions.

- Indicate the limits on the discussion: 'Let's spend ten minutes reviewing the situation before we start looking for a solution to this problem.'

Rule 6. Get things done

- People work best in comfortable, distraction-free rooms, so select your meeting room carefully.

- Keep to the agenda. Set clear objectives – don't get sidetracked. New items should be dealt with in general business or introduced as notices of motion for the next meeting.

> Achievements mark the success or otherwise of meetings. Ensure your objectives are met.

- Results often depend on the number of people involved. To solve a problem, fewer than five people is a good number.

  To identify a problem keep to 10 or less.

  When you need to review information, 20 should be the maximum. But for motivational or inspirational purposes the more the merrier, provided you have a good sound system.

- If you have a large group, make your meeting short and snappy. A small group of people can work around the clock to solve a problem but large numbers get restless because they cannot be involved to the same degree.

- People take a while to 'warm up' early in the morning. They watch the clock late in the afternoons and particularly before weekends.

  People tend to doze after large meals but after tea breaks they are refreshed. When you plan your agenda, important business should be introduced during peak periods of mental activity.

- Use visual aids to make a point and to increase your credibility.

- As leader you should be democratic but never lose control of a meeting. Be firm when necessary:

    'I don't wish to stifle discussion on this topic, but unless you want to be here until midnight let's keep to the agenda!'

Rule 7. Make the most of the talent and experience present

Use the special knowledge and expertise of your members to full effect.

- Often a free discussion for a few minutes when everyone can express their opinions stimulates new thinking and makes the most of experience at the meeting.

- If you are chairing, ask questions to draw out people with talent and experience.

    'Jim, do you agree with that point?'
    'Bill, is that your experience?'
    'Helen, how do you recommend we do the job?'

- For major issues, where time is limited, set up a compatible working party to collect facts, review the situation and bring down recommendations for the next meeting to consider.

- If you have an expert at the meeting, allow time to hear the expert's point of view but budget the time with clear directions:

    'We have five minutes to spare. Bill, let's hear the technical reasons why we should support this motion.'

Rule 8. Review and summarise often

Review progress periodically.

As leader it is your job to keep the meeting focused on agenda items.

Summarising is a key responsibility of the leader and mastery of this skill can help a chairperson conduct a very effective meeting. Once or twice during the meeting, review the proceedings and state how much of the agenda has been dealt with.

Summarise how far the group has progressed towards a decision and, if necessary, summarise individual contributions.

A final summary of the decisions reached can send members home with a sense of achievement.

Rule 9. Record recommendations and give members responsibilities for specific tasks

Often a great deal of the value of a meeting is lost because it is not clear who is responsible for tasks the meeting has agreed on. It is the leader's responsibility to make sure that the assignments are clear, the commitment is made, and follow-up action taken.

Record decisions and allocate tasks.

Minutes may seem very formal and time consuming but they are the assurance that the objectives of a meeting were achieved and the time was well spent. Concise minutes should be completed as soon as possible after the meeting. They are an essential part of the follow-up to see that things get done. Some minutes include simple statements of the following:

1. Conclusions reached
2. Items to be actioned and who is responsible
3. Matters unresolved.

More complete minutes may include a statement of:

1. Date, time, and location of the meeting
2. Objectives of the meeting
3. List of the participants
4. Matters discussed, item by item, including the opinions expressed by the people present
5. If the meeting involved voting, the names of those moving and seconding the motions, as well as the result of the vote
6. Tasks assigned, with expected results and dates
7. Matters on the agenda postponed or not considered, with an explanation.

Rule 10. Evaluate objectively

Analyse the meeting and what it achieved.

After the meeting, assess its success. Learn from this how to improve future meetings.

The best time to perform a 'post mortem' is soon after the meeting when you can still remember clearly what happened. Who came late? Who talked too much? Was anyone intimidated? Were there confrontations? Whose ideas were accepted or rejected? Note significant happenings. Decide how the next meeting can be improved and write yourself some reminders for next time.

Take a look at your agenda. Did you achieve your objectives?

Try to get informal feedback. A coffee break or social get-together is often a good opportunity to get some comments. Look for constructive criticism and try to act on it.

Aim to make each meeting better than the last.

A good chairperson is a good leader, so spend time preparing for the meeting and keep to the agenda. Try to remain impartial and not lose your temper. Use common sense. Review proceedings from time to time. Watch the time and guide the meeting accordingly to get things done.

Above all, remember the Golden Rule: 'Do unto others as you would have them do unto you.'

Then follow the ten simple rules outlined in this section.

'Will the meeting please come to order!'
'I declare this regular monthly meeting of . . . open for business.'

BRINGING ABOUT CHANGE USING FORMAL MEETING PROCEDURES

Do your homework

- Before you try to bring about changes in an organisation study its constitution, the bylaws, the amendments, the standing orders or whatever the meeting rules are called. Consult the rule book before you try to make changes.

- If you want to change procedures, read the section on procedural changes and stick to the 'letter of the law'.

- Study meeting procedures. Learn how to put a motion and how to 'gag' a motion. Know the motion procedures for the closure, the previous question and the next business. Beware of the term 'parliamentary procedures'. It is a loose term covering meeting procedures and it varies between authorities and countries. 'Robert's rules' are often quoted as the authority in the USA, as 'Renton's rules' are in Australasia. If 'parliamentary procedures' are quoted ask for a ruling from the chair – 'Whose procedures are we using?'

A thorough knowledge of a constitution is invaluable when you wish to make changes.

Lobbying

Informal meetings with committee members prior to a meeting can help to win support for or against a controversial motion. This can save a lot of time when the motion is introduced at the meeting.

Discuss contentious items beforehand with interested parties to save time at meetings and ensure motions are carried.

163

A GUIDE FOR CHAIRING A FORMAL MEETING

Agenda for a formal meeting

Procedural order.

1. Open the meeting
2. Apologies
3. Welcome new members and guests
4. Minutes of previous meeting
5. Matters arising from the minutes
6. Correspondence
7. Business arising from correspondence
8. Financial report
9. General business of which notice has not been given
10. Reports from committees
11. General business of which notice has been given
12. Other general business – with consent of the meeting
13. Notices of motions for future meetings
14. Announce date and time of next meeting
15. Close the meeting.

Opening the meeting

Make every effort to start on time. Rap a gavel to get attention, if you have one, and call the meeting to order:

'The meeting will come to order.'

Welcome the people present and declare the meeting officially open:

164

'I declare this regular [weekly, monthly, annual] meeting of the
. . . society open for business.'

This is an important statement because all business is recorded
from this point onwards.

The secretary will have checked the number of members to confirm
that a quorum is present. Names of members and guests are
recorded.

'Are there any apologies?'

Names of members who have asked to be excused attendance are
recorded. It should be moved:

'that the apologies be accepted.'

The chair then introduces new members and guests and makes a
short statement about the expectations of the meeting.

Minutes

'The secretary will read the minutes of the last meeting held at . . .
on . . . '

If the minutes have been circulated prior to the meeting they need
not be read. But ask for the motion: 'That the minutes be taken as
read.'

'Are there any corrections to the minutes?'

If not:

'The question is that I do sign these minutes as a true and correct
record.'

If this motion is carried, the chair then signs and dates the minutes.

If someone wants alterations made to the minutes, the meeting
must give its consent. If there are objections, a majority vote is
needed for the alterations to be made. The chair should initial
these.

Matters arising from the minutes

'Is there any business not on the agenda arising from the
minutes?'

Any matters which may have been overlooked or ignored can be discussed at this stage.

Correspondence

'Next the secretary/treasurer's report.'

The secretary reports on letters and communications received and sent, bills approved and paid and special happenings (such as visitors) not recorded in the minutes.

It is usual for the secretary to list letters received and sent. The meeting decides which ones are to be read out.

Business arising from the correspondence

Instructions should be given to the secretary, by a motion from the meeting, on action required.

When the correspondence has been dealt with it should be moved and seconded:

'That the inward correspondence be received and the outward correspondence be confirmed.'

Financial report

The constitution and bylaws will dictate how often the treasurer needs to present a full financial statement but it is a good practice to present a financial statement at monthly meetings. A formal motion is needed approving the list of accounts for payment. The regular monthly statement should be 'received'. The audited accounts should be 'adopted'.

General business of which notice has not been given

'Has any member any matters of general business which they wish to discuss later under general business?'

Calling for notice of general business at this stage will give the chair time to list matters of general business into a logical order and gives the meeting an idea of what yet remains to be discussed – it's a useful way of shortening a meeting.

Reports from committees

'We will now receive the committee reports. We will start with the conveners [see page 182] of the standing committees.'

Standing committees are set up to deal with regular and continuing business (eg a public relations committee). Reports should be in writing and are best circulated with the notice of the meeting.

'I now call for discussion or questions about this report.'

At the conclusion of the report the person who presents it should move: 'That the report be received' or 'That the report be adopted'. If 'received' the meeting is not committed to the recommendations. If 'adopted' the meeting is committed to support the recommendations.

General business of which notice has been given

Motions for which notice was given at a previous meeting or circulated prior to the meeting, with sufficient notice according to the bylaws, are discussed.

Other general business – with consent of the meeting

'Is there any other unfinished business? If not let us proceed to postponed business.'

The secretary or committee members remind the meeting of any postponed business.

'If there is no other postponed business we will consider new business.'

New topics should only be discussed with the consent of the meeting. Contentious and important matters should not be raised here.

Notices of motions for future meetings

There should be no discussion on future motions, only formal statements of intent that a motion will be presented at the next or at some future meeting.

Announce date and time of next meeting

The date and arrangements for the next meeting should be discussed, even though a notice will be sent out.

Close the meeting

'The business for this meeting has been completed. A motion for adjournment is now in order.'

The motion is put and seconded.

'It has been moved and seconded that this meeting be adjourned. All those in favour say "Aye," opposed "No." The motion is carried. I declare this meeting stands adjourned until our next regular meeting on . . .'

Read *Effective Meeting Skills* by Marion E Haynes (Kogan Page).

MOTION PROCEDURES MADE EASY

A motion is a formal proposal, suggestion or recommendation that something be done. Ideally it should be presented in writing. It should be expressed in simple terms and short sentences. It starts with the words 'I move that . . .'.

Seconding a motion

Most motions must be seconded. This is to make sure there is support for the proposal. Otherwise it would be a waste of time discussing it. The words used are 'I second the motion'. The seconder then has two alternatives: to speak immediately in support of the motion or to defer until later in the debate. If the latter, the seconder must add 'And I reserve the right to speak later'.

If no one seconds the motion, the chair must declare the motion 'lapsed for want of a seconder' and proceed to the next business.

Seconding is not required for motions (such as the closure) which are not debated, or for motions with which the chair agrees.

Debating a motion

When a motion has been seconded it is open to debate, and changes can be made to it. The chair asks the proposer to speak for the motion and then others are invited to give their opinions. With controversial issues it is usual to allow at least two speakers to speak against the motion. The proposer also has the right of reply at the end of the debate, to summarise arguments and to try and gain support for the motion. When the debate is concluded the chair puts the motion to the vote.

The vote

If everyone votes for the motion it is carried 'unanimously'. If more people vote for it than against it, it is carried 'by the majority'. If more people vote against it, it is 'defeated'. Once a motion has been approved by a majority it becomes a *resolution.*

Motion procedure

1. *Mover of motion* rises, announces the motion
2. *Chair* asks for seconder, if appropriate
3. *Seconder of motion* rises and seconds the motion
4. *Mover of motion* speaks for the motion
5. *Seconder of motion* speaks for the motion or reserves the right to speak later
6. *Speakers from the floor* speak for or against the motion
7. *Mover of motion* has the right of reply
8 *Secretary* reads the exact words of the motion
9. *Chair* puts the vote and announces results – carried or defeated.

Amendment to a motion

1. *Mover of amendment* rises and announces amendment
2. *Chair* asks for seconder
3. *Seconder of amendment* rises and seconds the amendment
4. *Mover of amendment* speaks for the amendment
5. *Seconder of amendment* speaks for the amendment
6. *Speakers from the floor* speak for or against the amendment
7. *Mover of motion* has the right of reply
8. *Secretary* records and reads the motion and amendment
9. *Chair* puts the amendment to the vote
   If carried, takes a vote on the amended motion
10. *Secretary* records the motion, amendment and result
11. If amendment is lost *chair* takes the vote on the original motion
12. *Secretary* records motion, amendments and result.

Tips

- The mover or the seconder of a motion may not move or second an amendment to their motion.

- Amendments may not be direct negatives to the original motion – they are to amend the motion, not do away with it.

- Motions and amendments can be withdrawn only with the consent of the mover, the seconder and the majority.

- Confusing amendments are best handled by isolating points of conflict. Deal with the general before the specific. Bring the main motion and amendments together and deal with each point of conflict separately.

Procedural motions (formal motions)

A procedural motion is one dealing with the conduct of the meeting; for example:

'That the meeting do now adjourn.'
'That Mr Ross be now heard.'

Procedural motions are used to interrupt or cut short a debate. There are two common procedural motions: 'That the question [the motion] be now put' and 'That the meeting proceed to the next business'.

They can be moved during debates and take precedence over the debate.

Procedural motions are accepted at the discretion of the chair. They can be moved only by persons who have not moved, seconded or spoken to the notice or amendment under discussion.

Table 39.1 lists the main ones.

Table 39.1 *Procedural motions*

Motion	Effect of motion	Seconder	Interrupt speaker?	Debatable?	Amendable?	If carried	If lost
Adjourn the meeting 'I move that the meeting be adjourned'	Terminates meeting. May additionally state time and place of next meeting. Applies to motions and amendments	Yes	No	Yes	Only to time, date and place	Adjourn meeting immediately	Discussion resumes
The closure 'I move that the motion be now put'	Terminates discussion and brings matter to the vote. Applies to both motions and amendments	No	Yes	No	No	Put the motion or amendment immediately	Discussion resumes
Question lie on table 'I move that the question lie on the table'	Suspends discussion on matter before meeting. Applies to motions and amendments. If carried, main motion and amendment, if any, are laid aside	Yes	No	No	No	Next business	Discussion resumes
Adjourn debate 'I move that the debate be adjourned'	Another method of shelving matter before meeting. Applies to motions and amendments. If carried, the amendment and original motion are both adjourned	Yes	No	Yes	Only as to time, date and place	Proceed to next business	Discussion resumes
Proceed to next business 'I move that the meeting proceed to the next business'	Postpones for the time being the matter before the meeting. Applies to motions and amendments	Yes	No	No	No	On motion proceed to next business; on amendment proceed with original motion	Discussion resumes
The previous question 'I move that the question be not now put'	Prevents a vote being taken on or shelves motion for that meeting. Applies to motions, not to amendments	Yes	No	Yes	No	Proceed immediately to next business	Put the original motion immediately without discussion or amendment

◀ 40. ▶

GUIDELINES FOR THE SECRETARY OF A MEETING

This chapter deals with the duties and responsibilities of a meeting secretary: how to send out notices of a meeting, write an agenda, keep minutes and action matters arising from the meeting.

The secretary's tasks

The efficient organisation and conduct of a meeting depend largely on the secretary and chairperson working as a team.

The success of a meeting may depend as much on the secretary as on the chairperson.

The secretary is the administrative officer of the organisation or committee and is responsible for ensuring decisions made at a meeting are implemented and that routine administrative work is carried out. Secretaries should be completely impartial in their duties and at meetings they should help the chairperson as much as possible.

The secretary can boost the morale of the organisation by ensuring the work of the committee is done quickly and efficiently. All routine business must be attended to promptly and decisions implemented. Clear and concise reports keep members well informed so there is good communication between the chairperson and committee and the organisation as a whole.

Preparing for a meeting

First, ensure the venue is suitable and available. Check that the place and time are convenient for most committee members.

Preparation.

Then prepare the *Notice of Meeting*. This should:

1. State the date, time and place of meeting.
2. Indicate the nature of the business. Include an agenda if possible.
3. Be clear and well set out.
4. Be issued on proper authority.
5. Be sent to all those entitled to get it.

Make every effort to give members early notice of meetings. Before the agenda is sent out, discuss it and have it approved by the chairperson.

The secretary can help by preparing a special agenda for the chairperson. This should include facts and figures, areas of conflict and constitutional guidelines.

Background papers

Background information.

If there are contentious or complicated items scheduled for a meeting, much time can be saved by preparing detailed background papers and circulating these well before the meeting.

A subcommittee or working party is often asked to prepare a background paper; sometimes the job is given to the secretary. If you are asked to prepare a background paper, collect the facts objectively, write them up logically and give conclusions and recommendations.

Before the meeting

Action before the meeting.

- Make sure the room is still available.
- Collect the key.
- Set out pads, pens, gavel, water and glasses.
- Make sure a lectern, projector and boards are available, if required. Don't forget chalk, duster and marker pens.
- If reporters are to be present, provide a table, positioned so that they can hear well, and near an exit.
- Keep a copy of the rules or constitution handy. If they are wordy, tabulate them for quick reference.
- Help the chairperson welcome guests and see they are looked after.

During the meeting

1. Sit next to the chairperson so that you can see and hear all that occurs and advise the chairperson, if necessary.

   Conduct of the meeting.

2. Have on hand all necessary documents, including minutes of previous meetings and a copy of the rules or constitution.

3. Record the names of those present (or circulate a paper for them to write their names on). Record apologies for absence.

4. Read the minutes of the previous meeting. Make sure they are signed and dated by the chairperson after they have been passed by the meeting as 'a true and correct record'. If the minutes have been circulated before the meeting, they are often 'taken as read'.

5. Report on correspondence.

6. Record the meeting in its proper sequence, especially the names of movers and seconders of resolutions.

7. Record motions correctly. Be prepared to repeat the motion to the chairperson, if required. Often the chairperson will ask the mover to submit the motion in writing.

8. If a motion is not seconded, draw the chairperson's attention to the need for a seconder. The chairperson should be encouraged to name the mover and the seconder, as you might be writing and not see them.

9. Resolutions must be reported in full. It is not necessary to record a motion that is proposed but fails because it was not seconded.

10. You *must* record when amendments to a motion are moved and withdrawn. You must record any amendments moved to a motion and carried, and then when the amendment is put as the motion and carried.

11. Record the results of votes taken.

Don't be afraid to make suggestions that could help the chairperson. Don't interfere in policy making or try to influence the committee's decisions. You can, however, tell the chairperson if a proposed action is forbidden under the constitution or impracticable because of lack of funds. *You must act on resolutions, even if you disagree with the decisions.*

The minutes

What the minutes should say.

The minutes of a meeting are a written record of the business discussed and decisions made at the meeting. When signed they become the permanent record of the proceedings. It is usual for them to be circulated before a meeting and confirmed as to their accuracy at the following meeting, then signed by the chairperson as a true and correct record. Minutes:

- Tell those who did not attend the meeting what happened
- Give future officers and members a better understanding of the affairs of the organisation
- Preserve continuity in debates
- Are available as evidence in legal proceedings
- Are available for auditing purposes
- Are available (subject to the rules of the organisation) for inspection by members.

After the meeting

Write up the minutes immediately after the meeting and before you attend to other business arising from the meeting. This helps to eliminate errors and omissions. The minutes should record:

- The name, place, date and hour of the meeting.
- The names of members present and apologies for non-attenders. This is required to prove a quorum was present. (A quorum is the number set down in the rules which must be present for the meeting to act legally.) There may also be penalties for non-attendance.
- The names of distinguished guests or others present by invitation.
- The names of committee members who arrive late or leave before the meeting closes – note the time of arrival or departure.
- The names of persons who vote against a resolution, if they request it.
- The *precise* words of every resolution.
- Any questions dealing with the appointment, duties, powers, or other rules of the organisation.
- All instructions to any members and all transactions authorised or ratified at the meeting.
- The time the meeting closed and the date and venue of the next meeting.

Refer the first draft of the minutes to the chairperson for approval or amendment before you prepare the final draft – especially if contentious issues have been discussed.

Alterations to minutes

Never erase minutes. Incorporate corrections into the minutes of the next meeting. Thus, 'The minutes of the meeting held on 10 July were approved subject to . . .'

Precautions against falsification of minutes

Take care that no one can alter the minutes in or out of the meeting. A good idea is to have a typed copy glued into a bound book. Number the pages of the minutes consecutively. Keep the minutes in a safe place.

Action arising from the minutes

As soon as possible after a meeting write memos and letters as indicated in the minutes to ensure follow-up action is taken.

Advise and remind people of their appointment to subcommittees and supply information promised at the meeting.

How to become a good secretary

What the good secretary needs to know.

- Learn the aims of the organisation.
- Know the constitution.
- Learn business procedures.
- Take brief notes. It is impossible to follow all the proceedings of a meeting if you write copious notes.
- Get things done promptly. The longer you put things off the harder they are to do.
- Write clear letters.

As secretary you have an important task. You are the oil in the machinery of your organisation, keeping it running smoothly.

◀ 41. ▶

ARRANGING TABLES FOR A MEETING

Avoid theatre-type seating unless it is a large meeting. For small meetings it is desirable to have participants seated at tables so they can take notes and have reference materials handy.

Figure 41.1 shows some table arrangements for small meetings. The arrangements will depend on the type of meeting, the size and shape of the room, the numbers attending and the number of available tables.

Rectangular tables can be placed together to make many combinations or separated for small working groups. Make sure everyone can see the chairperson and other participants.

For a small meeting (8–10 people) a round table is ideal. No one is obviously in the position of authority – all members are on an equal 'level' and this leads to good interaction between members.

Some conference rooms have tables which can be arranged in a hexagon (H) or two can be placed together to make a very convenient smaller table (I).

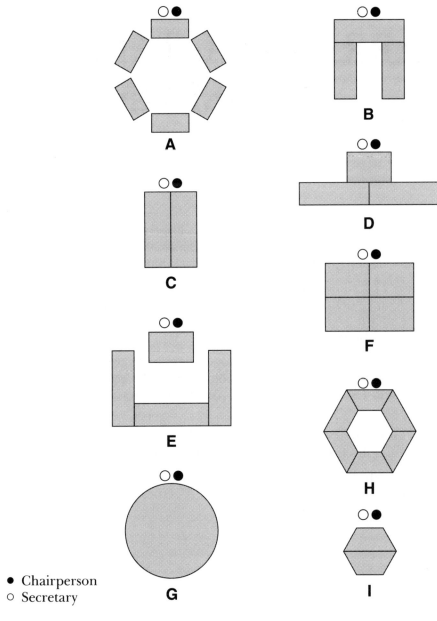

• Chairperson
○ Secretary

Figure 41 1 *Table arrangements for small meetings*

◄ 42. ►

SURVIVAL GLOSSARY FOR NEW OFFICE HOLDERS

Abstain
Decline to use one's vote.

Acclamation
Clapping. Used for votes of thanks and motions admitting new members.

Ad hoc committee
Special committee set up for a particular task.

Adjourn
Break off a meeting to resume later.

Agenda
List of items of business to be considered.

Amendment
Change proposed to a motion.

Annual accounts
Statements of income and expenditure for the year, to be audited and approved by the annual general meeting.

Annual general meeting (AGM)
Meeting of organisation held each year usually to elect office bearers and a committee and to approve the annual report and annual accounts, appoint auditors for the coming year and debate future direction and policy.

Annual report
Report on year's activities written and presented by the president, chairperson or chief executive of the organisation.

Auditor
Accountant appointed at the annual general meeting to check the annual accounts.

Ballot
Vote, usually secret, using paper voting slips or black and white marbles (rather than show of hands).

Call to order
Call by the chair to start a meeting or a request during the meeting for members to behave properly.

Casting vote
Vote cast by the chair to resolve a tie (equal number of votes for and against). The chair can choose not to use it on a contentious issue where impartiality is important.

Chair's action
Authority of the chair to deal with routine or urgent matters between meetings.

Challenge to the chair
Effort to overturn the chair's ruling.

Composite motion
Motion combining several motions on the same topic.

Constitution
Statement of the objectives and conduct of an association.

Convene
Call a meeting, assemble. *Convenor*: person who calls a meeting.

Coopted member
Person appointed to a committee by the existing members, usually because of certain skills or influences.

Debate
Discussion or argument.

Declaration of interest
Statement that a member is personally involved, usually financially, in the issue being discussed.

Delegate
Person sent by an association to represent it at another meeting.

Delegated powers
Powers handed down to a working party or an office bearer to act on behalf of a committee or meeting.

Division
Accurate count of voters, either by a show of hands or a body count, if an oral vote is not decisive.

Drafting amendment
Amendment that tidies up wording of a motion.

Ex officio
Put on a committee because of an office or post held.

Floor
When the chair gives a person permission to 'take the floor' they can address the meeting through the chair.

Floor member
Member who does not hold office.

Gavel
Mallet used by the chair to call for order or attention.

General business
Discussion on motions for which notice was given at previous meeting, short announcements, etc.

General meeting
Meeting of all members. 'Special' or 'extraordinary' general meetings can be called to deal with urgent business on major issues.

Guillotine
Decision made in advance to cut off a debate at a set time.

Mandate
Authoritative command, order.

Matters arising
Item on an agenda from a previous meeting, for reporting to current meeting.

Minutes
Record of meeting. Usually lists who was present, apologies,

motions, resolutions, amendments, decisions and persons responsible for carrying out decisions. They should be approved by the following meeting, signed by the chair and kept in a minute book.

Motion
Formal recommendation put to a meeting for debate and consideration. (It becomes a *resolution* when passed.)

Next business
'That the meeting proceed to the next business.' Tactic for disposing of a motion. Must be put to the vote immediately – no seconder required and no discussion.

Notice of motion
Formal statement of intent that a motion will be presented at the next or some future meeting.

Null and void
Invalid. A resolution may be voted 'null and void' if it is passed contrary to the constitution or bylaws.

On the floor
The meeting is considering a specific motion.

Orders of the day
Agenda. List of business to be discussed.

Other business, other general business
Item to deal with business not on the agenda. (Major or controversial business should not be raised here.)

Out of order
Not in accordance with rules or standing orders.

Point of information
Tactic to interrupt a meeting to correct or add to what a speaker is saying.

Point of order
Device for members to check the conduct of the meeting. Question directed at the chair for an answer or ruling.

Previous question
Used when you don't want a vote taken on a motion. 'I move that the question not now be put.' (It does not deal with business previously debated and voted on.)

Proposer
Person or delegation who proposes the motion or amendment and speaks first. The *mover*.

Proxy
Person authorised to act for another.

Proxy vote
Vote cast on behalf of another unable to attend.

Question be put
Motion which interrupts a meeting to propose that the vote be taken immediately.

Quorum
Minimum number who must be present at a meeting before business can be conducted. The number is usually laid down in the constitution or bylaws.

Refer back
A meeting can 'refer back' or return a report to a committee and ask them to reconsider. (Often it is a polite rejection.)

Reference motion
'That this matter be referred to a committee.' The motion often contains explicit instructions.

Resolution
Motion which has been approved for action.

Right of reply
Summing up by the mover at the end of the debate.

Seconder
Person who gives formal support to a motion. Main supporter of the proposer. (Speaks immediately after the proposer or after the opposer.)

Standing committee
Committee set up to deal with regular and continuing business.

Standing orders
Rules by which meetings are conducted (as distinct from the major principles which are set out in the constitution and bylaws).

Subcommittee
Committee or working party set up by a committee to examine a matter in depth.

Substantive motion
Main motion (as distinct from amendments proposed to it).

Table or *lay on the table*
Bring reports or documents to the notice of the meeting officially.

Tabling motion
'That the question lie on the table' is used to delay action by adjourning the debate.

Taken in parts
Motion is voted on, section by section.

Terms of reference
Instructions for a committee, subcommittee or working party.

Ultra vires
Beyond the powers of an organisation. (An activity not within the scope of the constitution is ultra vires and cannot be carried out. A motion may be ultra vires if inadequate notice had been given.)

Unanimous
Everyone present agrees.

Withdrawal of motion
The proposer, with the consent of the seconder, can withdraw a motion if the meeting gives its unanimous consent.

◀ 43. ▶

ORGANISING A LARGE CONFERENCE OR CONVENTION

Before you start

Before you start organising the conference or convention, answer these questions: **Preparation.**

1. Why is the conference being held?
2. What are the aims of the organisation and the objectives of the meeting?
3. Who do you hope will attend?
4. How many people will you be able to accommodate?

If you are the organiser, your job is to coordinate. You don't do all the work – you delegate jobs to others. You act as the link or the memory of the organisation.

Select a good working committee made up of people who have time to do things and get things done. Call an initial meeting of these people if they have agreed to take responsibilities. Give each person clear written instructions:

> 'You are responsible for all publicity. Your job is to . . . You have the power to set up your own working party and to delegate jobs to others. But you are responsible for seeing things get done and for reporting progress at the scheduled meetings of the organising committee.'

Selecting a theme

Make sure the theme of the conference is relevant. It should deal **The subject.**

187

with topical issues and present new and stimulating ideas; for example:

'Profitability for survival'
'Changes needed for the next decade'.

Choosing speakers

Speakers.

For a large conference, lasting say two days, you may need at least 15 speakers. You require a great deal of information from your speakers and some of this (eg the subject) can be obtained early. Other information, such as travel arrangements and accommodation requirements, cannot be obtained until nearer the conference date. Unless you make up a checklist, it is easy to forget to book accommodation for a speaker. Even if someone else is making all the bookings and travel arrangements for speakers, the organiser must have a full list easily available.

Basic considerations when choosing a speaker are:

- You must know what topic you want discussed. Be specific.
- You must know how your speaker will perform on the selected topic.
- You must know how the speakers will fit into the pattern of your conference. Will they be compatible with your audience? Have they good local knowledge? Will they draw people?

Once your draft programme has been prepared, telephone each speaker (person-to-person) to tell them the objectives and dates of the conference and invite them to present a paper. With luck your programme will be finalised within half a day.

If you write to each speaker it may take months to finalise your programme. This can seriously affect advertising and consequently the number of people attending.

It is best to contact the speakers yourself. Most speakers prefer to deal with the organiser rather than an assistant.

Follow up the telephone calls immediately with letters confirming the discussion and giving speakers as much information as possible. This should include:

- Date and time of the meeting.

- Where the conference is to be held and how to find the building. (A simple map may be helpful.)
- Time of day when the speaker will have to perform (ie where the speaker will appear on the programme).
- How much time is available for the speech.
- Who will be at the conference (occupations, age groups etc).
- How many people you expect to attend.
- Who the other speakers will be.
- If the conference will be covered by newspaper, radio and television reporters.
- Time the conference will finish.
- Who will make accommodation and travel arrangements. (It may be possible at this stage to enclose travel tickets and details of accommodation.)
- What information the speaker would like to have included in publicity material and for the introduction at the meeting.
- Advising the speaker how he or she will fit into the pattern of the programme.

Remember, most failures are due to poor briefings rather than poor guest speakers.

Speakers are your guests
Treat each speaker as a welcome guest and do everything you can to make his or her stay a pleasant one.

On the day of the meeting double check that the speaker knows the procedures. Make sure good seats in the meeting room are available for speakers and guests. Introduce the speakers to the chairperson and the projectionist, and let them try out the sound system before the meeting starts.

After the meeting don't neglect the speakers. Follow through with your hospitality. Make sure someone sees them off and, if necessary, takes them to the airport or transport terminal.

Immediately after the meeting write a note of thanks to each speaker. Tell them how they helped you, mention any favourable comments you heard from people attending, and enclose any press cuttings they would be interested in.

How to prepare the programme
As soon as you get replies from your guest speakers, begin to   **The programme.**

prepare the programme. Leave gaps for local speakers who can discuss topical subjects that may arise later.

Always have a few emergency speakers on a reserve list. Often someone has business or personal emergencies and cannot attend the conference. When this happens, telephone the substitute, bring in a local speaker, or organise a panel or topical forum.

The programme should:

- Be 'eye catching' to attract the attention of the people you are trying to reach
- Arouse immediate interest
- Point out the benefits obtained by attending
- Give the place, the day, the time, and who you expect to attend.

Keep talk titles to basic English – no technical jargon. Make sure the titles tell exactly what the talk will about. If necessary, add a paragraph under the title setting out more details and adding information about the speaker. Subjects should be:

- Topical
- Interesting and relevant to the audience
- Give information which can be used.

A good subject is one that will benefit people who hear it or will help them overcome a problem. The question everyone asks is: 'What's in this for me?' A subject such as 'Investing your savings for greater returns' would probably have wide appeal.

Publicity

Publicity is essential. Good publicity is essential. But remember, good publicity alone may attract people to a poor meeting once, never twice. You must have an interesting, relevant, even controversial theme and good speakers.

For publicity purposes and good management make a master list of details about your speakers:

- Full name and correct initials
- Address
- Designation

- Qualifications
- Name of subject
- Has speaker confirmed in writing?
- Does he or she require accommodation?
- What sort of accommodation?
- When arriving
- When departing
- Where booked in
- How travelling
- Need to be met?

(It is often possible to arrange for a member of the organisation who is coming by private car to bring a guest speaker.)

You will require background information for an introduction to each paper and, if possible, a photo of each speaker. During the meeting copies of each paper, or summaries, should be available for press handouts.

Your conference and convention checklist

Conference checklist.

Accommodation
Agreement is needed with hotels or motels on:

- Approximate number of guest rooms needed, with details of singles, doubles, and suites
- Room rates
- Reservations confirmation
- Copies of reservations to those concerned
- Date that majority of group is arriving
- Date that majority of group is departing
- Date uncommitted guest rooms are to be released
- Rooms to be assigned to important guests
- Hospitality suites needed
- Cloakrooms, gratuities, bars, snacks, service time, and dates.

Meeting rooms
Figure 43.1 shows the ideal stage setting. Check with the conference centre, hotel or motel before the meeting on:

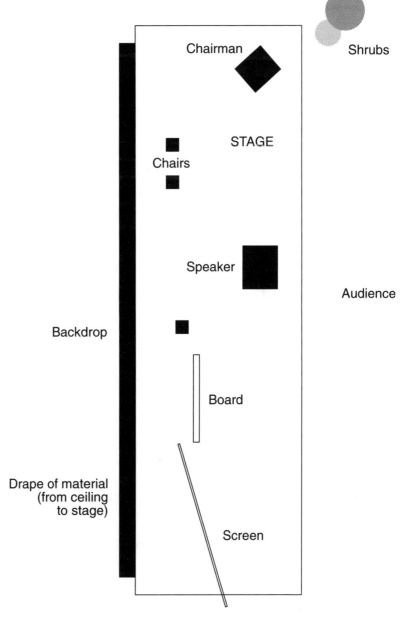

Figure 43.1 *An ideal stage setting*

- Floor plans
- Costs of rooms
- Dates and times for each session
- Rooms assigned for sessions
- Officials' room and room for the press
- Seating numbers, seating plan for each session, speakers' tables and press tables with lights
- Meeting schedules
- Staging required – size
- Special requirements
- Cloakroom
- Seating arrangements
- Enough seats for all
- Cooling or heating system operating
- Public address system operating
- Microphones – number and type
- Recording equipment operating
- Lectern in place, light operating, gavel and block available
- Water jug, water and glasses
- Door attendants
- Ashtrays, stands, matches (if smoking is permitted)
- Overhead projector and screen
- Pencils, notepads, paper
- Chart stands, easels, boards
- Signs, flags, banners
- Lighting as ordered
- Special flowers and plants as ordered
- Signs if meeting room is difficult to locate and signs for toilets
- Shorthand secretary
- Photographer
- Someone assigned to remove equipment after the meeting
- Arrangements for lost property.

Equipment and facilities
- Letterboxes for guest invitations, messages
- Equipment needed – availability, lists and prices
- Signs for registration desk, hospitality rooms, members only, tours, welcome notices
- Lighting – spots, floods, operators

- Staging – size
- Overhead projector and screen
- Blackboards, laminated boards, flannelboards, magnetboards
- Chart stands and easels
- Lighted lectern
- Gavel, block
- Public address sound system – microphones, types, number
- Recording equipment, operator
- Film or slide projection equipment, black-out switch
- Special flowers and plants
- Printing services
- Parking
- Decorations (check fire regulations)
- Special equipment
- Telephones
- Photographer
- Shorthand secretary
- Flags, banners
- Radio and television broadcasting
- Closed-circuit television.

Registration
- Time and days required
- Registration lists
- Registration cards – information required, number
- Tables – number, size
- Tables for filling out forms – number, size
- Hospitality desk
- Chairs
- Ashtrays
- Typewriters – number, type
- Personnel – their knowledge, procedures to be followed
- Water jugs, glasses
- Lighting
- Bulletin boards – number, size
- Signs
- Notepaper, pens, pencils, sundries
- Telephones
- Information on badges

- Arrangements for guests
- Programme and other material in place
- Wastepaper baskets.

Speakers

Check these things at least four weeks before the meeting:

- Have speakers been informed of the length of time available for them to speak?
- Have speakers been briefed on the type of talk desired?
- Are financial arrangements understood? Fee or expenses only? Fee or fee plus expenses? When is payment to be made?
- Are background articles and photographs available for publicity and introduction?
- Is speaker's spouse coming?
- Has hotel reservation been made?
- Will speaker require special equipment?
- Has speaker been furnished with the programme or draft programme?
- Has someone been designated to meet speaker upon arrival and to look after him or her until departure?
- Have letters been sent to confirm all arrangements?

Check immediately before meeting

- Has speaker been personally introduced to officials? Have special needs been met?
- Is board, easel etc in place?
- Are pointers and chalk in place?
- Will help be needed in turning charts?
- Is projector set up and tested?
- Is projectionist ready?
- Is there material to be given out?
- Will speaker need assistance?
- Are substitute speakers available in case of emergencies? (Forums and panels can help in an emergency.)

Decorations

- Have decorations and storage space for them been arranged?
- Have fire regulations and hotel policy been checked?

Entertainment
- Have entertainment programmes been planned?

Guests
- Have local dignitaries been invited?
- If they have accepted the invitation, have they been provided with tickets?
- Have they been forewarned about any speaking requirements?
- Have arrangements been made to welcome them?

Publicity
Refer to part publicity. Ask yourself the following:

- Has an effective publicity committee been set up?
- Have editors and radio and TV programme directors been informed personally of the aims and importance of the conference?
- Has a publicity programme been prepared?
- Have newsworthy press releases been prepared?
- Have arrangements for publicity photographs been made?

Recording
- Have arrangements been made to take minutes of the meeting, to type resolutions, to print proceedings?

Registration list
- Have arrangements been made to print registration lists?

Signs
- Have signs been prepared for: registration desk, hospitality room, tickets, information, members only, special events, committee, special tours, ladies' committee, no smoking, welcome, advance registration, press room?
- Have adequate signs been prepared to assure smooth operation?
- Is masking tape available for mounting the signs in appropriate places?

What type of advertising should you use?

Newspapers

Keep your newspapers well informed of developments, especially when guest speakers acknowledge invitations to speak. This is very effective free publicity.

Paid advertisements, especially big notices, are expensive. Often, if the programme is well publicised in other ways, several small advertisements may be better. Try to make them stand out by using a block or by using bold black lines around the advertisement. Select your days to advertise carefully. It is better to have your final advertisement the day before the event, rather than the week before. The advertising manager can advise on the best days to advertise.

Advertisements appearing in the public notice columns are usually seen before advertisements in adjoining columns.

Supplements

Newspaper advertising supplements are a good form of publicity, especially if they are free and the newspaper people do most of the work. Newspapers often run supplements for conferences. Some charge, others do not. Usually arrangements must be made early, with the advertising manager. Give full particulars and provide a number of programmes and publicity handouts, so that they can be used to sell advertising space to commercial organisations. This form of advertising involves a lot of copy about the conference, speakers, photographs, and so on. This is where early replies from the speakers help.

Television

Try to get free interviews on television if your guest speakers are newsworthy.

Radio

Use every opportunity to publicise your meeting and conference. Good publicity is obtained by arranging for a radio interview a few days before the event.

Paid advertisements
A few brief radio commercials near the weather forecast or news can be effective.

Hoarding
This is an effective and cheap form of publicity if placed on main thoroughfares. Watch out for regulations.

Signs and posters
These can be effective especially if well placed in shops, halls, foyers of firms and banks, and near office counters. Again, watch out for regulations.

Handouts
Handouts are cheap to print, but can be expensive to distribute if you have to mail them. Make them eye-catching. A cartoon on the cover or colourful printing will often encourage people to read on.

Here are some effective ways to get free distribution:

- Make them available on shop and office counters.
- Ask appropriate organisations to include them in local correspondence. Many such organisations will post them out with their notices of meetings or newsletters. Some firms will post them out with their accounts (or monthly statements) or just as a service to their clients.
- Distribute them at meetings.
- Get them inserted in the local newspaper.

Stamps and stickers
Rubber stamps or stick-on labels are cheap to prepare and can be used effectively on envelopes or outgoing mail.

Public relations office
Most local authority PR offices will publicise dates of local events if you plan far enough ahead.

Word of mouth

Word of mouth can be one of the most effective and cheapest forms of advertising. Get your friends or staff, when talking to clients, to invite them along. Address meetings and tell them about your conference. If you want support, always act enthusiastically and you will be surprised at the results.

Note

If you plan well in advance most of your advertising will be free, but don't spoil your conference for want of a few pounds in paid publicity.

The final check

Check these items to ensure smooth running of the conference.

Are the rooms ready?

- Make sure the auditorium hasn't been double booked.
- Will there be enough seats?
- Do you need to hire more?
- Do the lights and power points work?
- Do you know how to work all the switches?
- Can you work the ventilation and heating systems?

Advertising going well?

Are you getting comments from potential attenders? Better step up publicity with a few extra advertisements to make sure.

How about caterers?

Have you discussed on-the-spot arrangements with them? Do they have a working knowledge of times for serving food?

Are the speakers all coming?

What! Some couldn't make it? Don't panic! How about running an extra film or a forum or allowing extra time for questions. A brains trust is a good idea. Take three of your top speakers and ask them topical questions.

Have you plenty of helpers?
Do they all know what their jobs are?

Have you all the equipment ready:

- An adjustable lectern
- A large screen
- Projectors (check the lamps)?

Always have a few spare bulbs handy. Have you a flashing device for the speaker to indicate to the projectionist when to change slides? If you haven't, one can be made cheaply by a local electrician from a rectangular torch and a push button switch.

Have you checked the overhead projector?

Is there a pointer for speakers?

Tables
- You will need a table for the speaker, preferably with a cover on it and a vase of flowers.
- The press and broadcasting people will need tables.
- The projectionist will need a suitable table.
- The caterers will need tables.

Table lights
Lights will be needed for:

- The speaker
- The chairperson
- Reporters.

Small table lamps and two-way plugs can often be hired. Plenty of electric leads will be needed. Check they are safely taped down.

Make sure you have:
- Board, easel, duster, chalk
- A few sheets of soft-board, handy for pinning up signs
- Comfortable chairs for the stage
- Cardboard, newsprint and felt-tipped pens for making last-minute signs

- Name cards with ribbons, or stick-on labels for officials and speakers
- A jug of water and a glass for the chairperson's table
- Drawing pins, Sellotape, string
- Assorted tools
- A first aid kit.

Choose capable leaders

The success of a conference or a convention largely depends on the personalities and knowledge of the people chairing sessions.

Have you prepared notes for them? They should be sent details of the speakers' qualifications and backgrounds well before the conference. A good chairperson will study these notes at home and *not* read them out on the day.

Good leading speakers and chairpersons are essential for success.

Some last-minute checks

- Are you sure the sound system and projectors are available for the day?
- Are the transport arrangements for speakers checked?
- Are the displays all ready?
- Are you allowing people to smoke in the meeting rooms?
- Do you need help with car parking?
- Don't forget to obtain copies of the speakers' papers for the local and national press.

Check some final details and walk through the venue to ensure the planned routings are well signposted and accessible. You have done your best. Now relax and enjoy yourself.

After it's over

- Write to the speakers to thank them. Mention any feedback you have had on their performances and enclose any newspaper clippings which would interest them.
- Pay the accounts.
- Write your reports.
- Thank your assistants.
- How could we have done better? Give objective comments to help future organisers.
- Use copies of the papers presented (or main ideas from them) for post-conference publicity.

Finish the correspondence, pay the bills and evaluate the results. If appropriate, publish the papers.

◄ APPENDIX ►

TRY DIFFERENT WAYS TO GET YOUR IDEAS ACROSS

Most people have too few tools in their communication kit. There are many ways to get messages across to staff, clients or the public. Have you ever considered some of the following? It's not a complete list, but it might spark ideas.

- Advertisements in newspapers and magazines
- Advisory boards, subcommittees or working parties
- Alamanacs
- 'Alumni' activities which involve retired employees
- Anniversary books or brochures
- Announcement folders with photographs, biographical data etc when senior staff are appointed
- Ashtrays or coasters with messages
- Attitude surveys to allow employees or clients to express opinions (without identification) on policies, procedures, plans and practices
- Badges or cufflinks
- Balloons with messages
- Banners
- Billboards
- Birthday greetings
- Booklets offering services or information
- Books
- Brochures
- Bulletin boards for brief topical information to advise about events, stop rumours

- Bulletins to announce something of immediate concern
- Bus and train advertisements
- Calendars setting out events, containing messages
- Calling systems (used to locate employees)
- Campaigns
- Car stickers
- Cards (business, identification, visiting)
- Cartoons
- Charts
- Circulation of printed matter (or 'Please take one' containers)
- Civic activities
- Clubs for recreation or social activities
- Comics
- Committees
- Complaint boxes
- Computer letters or messages
- Conferences
- Contests (art, photographic, games, puzzles, quizzes, raffles, sales, writing, model making, safety etc)
- Counselling sessions
- Cup messages (slogans or logos on paper cups)
- Debates
- Demonstrations
- Diagrams
- Diaries with quotes, hints and facts about organisation
- Dictionaries
- Digests of articles, statements or reviews
- Direct mail
- Directories (employees, services, products, telephone)
- Discussion groups
- Displays
- Educational souvenirs
- Emergency cards or stickers
- Exhibits
- Fact cards – with a calendar on the back
- Family activities – visits to the office, picnics, sports days etc
- Field trips
- Film strips and slides
- Films
- Financial and annual reports

- Floor plans (especially if new building)
- Forums
- Glossaries of terms
- 'Grapevine' ('bush telegraph')
- Graphs, pie charts etc
- Grievance boxes
- Handbooks for new employees (history, organisation charts, benefits etc)
- History of the organisation
- Hoardings
- Holiday greetings – cards or booklets with useful information
- Identification cards
- In-service training
- Induction programmes
- Information reading racks
- Intercom systems
- Interviews
- Invoices with message slips attached
- Leaflets
- Lectures
- Letters
- Letters to the editors of newspapers and magazines
- Libraries
- Magazine articles and advertisements
- Manuals setting out organisation procedures, rules etc
- Maps showing location of buildings, services, parks etc
- Matchbooks or lighters with messages or slogans
- Meetings
- Memos
- Menu cards or place mats
- Museums – displays
- Nameplates
- Neon signs
- Newsletters
- Newspapers, articles and advertisements
- Notebooks with logos and information
- Open-house programmes
- Organisation charts
- Overhead projectors
- Panel discussions

- Paper pads with logos and/or commercials
- Paper serviettes, pens, pencils with messages
- Pay cheques with message slips attached
- Pay envelopes with messages or token gifts
- Photographs with captions
- Picture books
- Policy statements
- Postcards
- Posters
- Press releases
- Programmes for events (concerts, sports days etc)
- Public address systems
- Radio – interviews, commercials, news items, releases
- Readerships surveys
- Receptionist and reception areas
- Records and tapes
- Recreational activities
- Reports
- Reprints of articles
- Rubbish bag and bin advertising
- Rule books, lists of regulations, procedures, acts etc
- Rumour box or rumour board
- Samples of products
- Sandwich boards
- Seminars
- Service clubs
- Signs
- Skits
- Slides (35 mm)
- Slogans
- Social activities
- Souvenirs with logos (eg packet containing seeds from native flowering plant)
- Spectacle wipes – with a message
- Speeches
- Stickers for windows, car bumpers, coat lapels
- Suggestion prizes for good ideas
- Symposia
- T-shirts
- Tape recordings

- Taxi advertisements
- Tea towels
- Telephone messages, interviews and conference calls
- Telephone directories ('Yellow pages')
- Television – advertisements commercials, interviews, documentaries and news items, Ceefax/Teletext
- Time-clock cards
- Tours (plant, office, gardens, research stations etc)
- Training activities
- Tuition programmes
- Vacation kits (maps, first aid, sewing, shoe-cleaning etc)
- Videos
- Visits
- Washrooms – messages above handbasins, on backs of toilet doors
- Workshops

Further Reading

The Business Guide to Effective Writing, JA Fletcher and DF Gowing
Improving Your Communication Skills, Malcolm Peel
Readymade Business Letters, Jim Dening
Talk is Cheap, Godfrey Harris with Gregrey Harris

A full list is available from Kogan Page, telephone 071-278 0433.

INDEX